NATASHA COURTENAY-SMITH

THE MILLION DOLLAR BLOG

piatkus

PIATKUS

First published in Great Britain in 2016 by Piatkus

Copyright © Natasha Courtenay-Smith 2016

3 5 7 9 10 8 6 4

A CIP catalogue record for this book
is available from the British Library.

ISBN 978-0-349-41406-5

Typeset in Miller by M Rules
Printed and bound in Great Britain by
Clays Ltd, St Ives plc

Papers used by Piatkus are from well-managed forests
and other responsible sources.

Piatkus
An imprint of
Little, Brown Book Group
Carmelite House
50 Victoria Embankment
London EC4Y 0DZ

An Hachette UK Company
www.hachette.co.uk

www.improvementzone.co.uk

THE
MILLION
DOLLAR
BLOG

CONTENTS

Prelude

The place is Soho, London. The event is London Fashion Week and the biggest buzz comes from . . . well, *not* as you might expect, from the catwalk . . .

The scene's familiar – the crème de la crème of the global fashion industry hitting the streets, flocking from show to show dressed in their most striking ensembles, fingers glued to their iPhones as they update their social media at every turn.

But today there's a different type of buzz in the air – the buzz of the new VIPs in the fashion world. Where once there were magazine editors and photographers, the power players of fashion, sitting in the front rows and being wooed by designers, now there is a new breed of influencers . . .

. . . the Fashion Bloggers – and they've even got their own celebrity 'zone'.

'The Apartment' is a pop-up fashion week workspace for the exclusive use of 150 of the world's most influential bloggers. With its clean, white decor, its café catered by Aubaine and shelves piled high with coconut water and spritzers, it's a modern day fusion of luxury hotel and designer office.

In the main room, everything needed to create and edit content is on tap – from computers loaded with the latest editing software to cutting edge smartphones and tablets provided by Three. A live stream of the catwalk shows is projected onto the walls and, defying the uncomfortable conventions of normal offices, the star-status bloggers are ensconced in deep leather sofas and Eames rocking chairs.

The VIP treatment doesn't end there. Over in the Beauty studio, Mark Hill, one of the UK's most famous hairdressers, is on hand with his team to offer the 150 hand-picked bloggers a range of VIP styling experiences. Standing by are other leading brands ready to fit eyelash extensions and polish nails. In The Showroom, brands such as Urban Outfitters, Boden and Genevieve Sweeney have loaned a selection of clothes and accessories for bloggers who know the value of presenting themselves in at least three different outfits during the day.

It's not just a London phenomenon . . .

Similar scenes unfolded at New York Fashion Week, where influential fashion bloggers such as Bryanboy and Leandra Medina could be seen in privileged front row positions in the catwalk shows, alongside the traditional power-players such as *Vogue* editor Anna Wintour.

And why? It's not just that they share the same huge audiences enjoyed by the traditional media, such as print magazines, TV shows or newspapers – it's because they have the *keenest* audiences too. These top fashion bloggers are vocal, likeable and authentic, with a lack of bias and no need to follow anyone's rules but their own – this is why they connect with their audience more powerfully than a regular media outlet might.

Not surprisingly, brands are paying attention. The brands have had to sit there while people increasingly flick over or generally ignore their advertisements in magazines, even when they have shelled out for the best photographers and models. They see what is going on – and they want a piece of that reach, influence and engagement.

Brands who happily spent millions a year with traditional outlets are now doing so with bloggers and the contracts are getting more lucrative with every year. In 2016, a new bar was set when fashion blogger Kristina Bazar – whose blog *Kayture* (kayture.com) is the most influential blog in Switzerland and has increasing influence around the world – secured a contract with L'Oréal, said to be worth seven figures a year, and she's only 21!

As Yann Joffredo, vice president of global cosmetics at L'Oréal, said: 'She is a bridge between classical advertising and the consumer. Kristina is totally in line with all the values of the brand.' Of course, it helps too that she has nearly two and a half million Instagram followers and her blog gets over two million visitors per month!

It's not just happening in the fashion world

Across the blogosphere it is the fashion and lifestyle bloggers who are perhaps the most visible and well known. They are the online equivalent of Hollywood stars in the mainstream media – the ones who seem to lead the best lives, get to do the best things and who seem to have the world at their feet.

It's the modern day rags to riches tale – someone who has made the journey from nobody to somebody – and it would have been nothing but a pipedream if not for their laptop and their ability to type. They show that a young person can use just opinions and content creation to rise to the top of an industry – fashion – that has always seemed completely impenetrable.

But fashion blogging is just one part of the huge and profitable blogosphere. Whatever you do, whoever you are, whatever you're interested in, whatever you know about, whatever business you run, blogging can help you and change your life.

Blogging is an evolving force

Blogging isn't new. Chapter 2 touches on the history – where it all started and how it's evolved – but today's fashion bloggers show just how far it's come. No longer simply a means of publishing your opinions to a website, as it was 10 years ago, now ever-fiercer competition for attention amongst news organisations, brands, celebrities, and your mate who blogs about their kid's table manners, means it's never been tougher to be a real standout success in the digital storytelling landscape.

So in a world where everyone wants to blog and blog posts are ubiquitous, how do you stand out? How do you blog your way from nobody to somebody? How do you, as a business owner, use content to build your brand, your profile and drive your success?

In this book, I'll be taking you on a journey through the philosophies, strategies and journeys of some of the world's greatest bloggers who have shared their stories with us. I will also be covering practical and theoretical aspects of blogging – although this book is not a step-by-step guide to the technical side of setting up a blog. Instead, I'd like to give you an overarching view and understanding of the blogosphere, the opportunities it contains for both individuals and business owners. You'll hear from those who have created lifestyles way beyond their imaginations thanks to their blog.

No matter who you are – a mum at home, a budding fashion blogger, or a small business owner – you'll learn the philosophies, strategies and 'big picture' behind successful blogging. Whether you are someone who wants to start a blog but has no idea how to begin, someone with a fledgling blog who wants to take it to the next level, whether you work as a freelance service provider, an expert, or the owner of a business, large or small, wondering how content and blogging can help you grow your business, get more customers and position yourself as the leader in the field, then this book is for you.

Although text-led blogging via a website is at the heart of the book (and I believe, at the heart of all successful blogs whether they are blogstar blogs, personal blogs, expert blogs or business blogs) we'll also be talking about personal branding, vlogging and social media too – as in today's interconnected, social, conversational world, the success and profile of your blog is inextricably linked to your overall positioning both in terms of your site AND your success across the giant social platforms of today. In our pursuit of a million dollar blog, it is not possible to separate any part from the other and pursue it singly. Instead, all aspects of the online world must be pursued together, as you shall see, and you will most likely find yourself creating different forms of content for your blog and for your social media channels.

Whatever your goal, you're about to learn how to harness the power of content to increase your profile, create new opportunity, earn money and eventually achieve superstardom.

PART ONE

Prelaunch

You've decided you're going to become a blog star, or use blogging to build your business or profile. You might already have a blog or a personal profile that you want to build. Brilliant! Because if there is one step or activity in this world that enables and empowers you to take control of your life and head in an entirely new direction, or take a small idea and turn it into a giant one, it is creating content and building digital visibility.

So, all you need to do is sit at your computer and start typing, right? Well, while the answer is 'yes' on one level, on another it's not quite so simple. You see, success online does not come from a single dimension or action. It is multifaceted and multilevelled and you need to look at it and understand it from all sorts of different angles.

Part 1 of this book is all about laying down the framework that you'll need for online success. Many bloggers trying to build their blogs do not have the 360-degree perspective you're about to gain, or if they do, they have stumbled upon it via trial, error and accident. Enjoy.

Chapter 1

A day in the life of a Blog Star
(and 13 reasons why YOU should blog)

Mankind's greatest migration

Thanks especially to the highly visible fashion and lifestyle bloggers, blogging has become the 'it' career of the modern world.

A recent survey (2014) revealed that 25 per cent of under-25s in the UK regard blogging as their career of choice (compared to just 14 per cent who chose sport and only 9 per cent who selected politics). The 2014 survey went on to analyse the range of beliefs that make blogging so attractive:

- Bloggers don't have to do much work (29 per cent of respondents).
- Bloggers earn good money (22 per cent).
- Bloggers are admired by other people (19 per cent).
- Blogging is easy (16 per cent).

The stats bear this out. In the UK alone there are over 100,000 Google searches each month on topics such as 'How to blog' and 'Can I start a blog?' And globally, 50,000 blogs are launched per day just on the WordPress platform. In fact, most of us know someone who wants to blog or thinks they should be blogging, or who has indeed already tried it.

Celebrity culture has had to expand to include this new breed, the 'blog star' – bloggers who are so successful that they are millionaires, attracting as much attention as more conventional celebrities. This celebrity status is continually reaffirmed by the star appearances (with star-sized fees) and the designer goods, complimentary air fares and luxury accommodation all offered by the brands they comment on to the most influential of these bloggers.

Lucrative blogging is not, however, confined to the world of luxury and celebrity. In the business world everyone is using content marketing (the discipline of creating quality content for your brand or business to engage potential purchasers, strengthen brand loyalty and spread your message – aka *blogging for business*), and this market is now worth a staggering £4 BILLION in the UK alone.

Businesses either employ outside agencies to create their content or, with the real leaders such as Burberry, they have developed their own content studio to create endless content for their websites and social media, which in turn drives sales and leaves their offline counterparts far behind. Coca Cola's online magazine 'Journey' (aka their content strategy) has twenty-four separate online editions around the globe, and millions of readers per month, with consistent viral success.

Meanwhile, business professionals from GPs and fitness instructors to management consultants and PR professionals are using blogging to improve their expert standing, authority and visibility in their industry.

What's drawn YOU to this book?
(and 13 reasons to start blogging!)

From fashion to professional services, blogging can be hugely profitable, so whatever your reason it's not at all surprising that you've ended up with this book in your hands. But you may still be far from convinced or from understanding how exactly blogging converts into cash or where the true benefits of blogging lie. So let's outline right now 13 powerful reasons to start blogging ...

The simple route to creating your own business

1. Blogging is easy

During much of this book I will be talking about how becoming a high-earning celebrity blogger is not easy – but the process of blogging itself is very easy and, in terms of setting up a small business, starting blogging has to be about as easy as it gets.

Most businesses require money to get started, whether for stock, tools or even a lease or property. But you can start a WordPress blog for free, or choose to have one with your own branded domain name for less than £100. Setting up the basic framework for your blogs takes very little time and you don't even need your own laptop (although life will be a lot easier with one, and computer equipment just gets cheaper every year).

So, the barriers to entry for blogging are minimal, and the success stories are so astounding that it's difficult to think of a reason not to give it a go.

A chance to improve your lifestyle

2. You can make money

I should know – I did it!

In 2008 I started blogging as a strategy for the business I then owned, which was one of the UK's leading online press agencies, called Talk to the Press. In short, the business provided publicity and media management for ordinary people wanting to share their story with the national papers, magazines and television.

Over the years, we helped thousands of ordinary people manage press attention in their lives, get featured in women's magazines or national newspapers, see their stories turned into books, appear on TV programmes or documentaries. We were responsible for dozens of front page newspaper stories and some of our clients went on to deliver real change, such as seeing laws changed on issues such as child abuse. The agency also won numerous awards and saw me feature on *Management Today*'s prestigious '35 under 35' list of high flying women in the UK, and win the 'Women in Business' category at the Startups Awards.

So, how did we do all of this? Well, quite simply, through blogging. We published blog posts on our area of expertise, our success stories, images from behind the scenes of the business, talking, showing and demonstrating how we could help, and how we were helping people, twice a week, and all sorts of good things happened.

Our Google position rose until we ranked top of Google for all the keywords that would bring in new leads to the business. The overall impression of the business upon hitting its website was that it was trustworthy and full of integrity (and this is at a time when no one really trusted journalists at all!) and, within the industry, the business became regarded as the best in its sector – we won awards. Over the years, my blogging strategy for the business brought in several million dollars in total sales and clearly positioned us as a leader in the industry. In 2014 I was able to sell the business (along with its blog) in its entirety.

But trust me, my success story is small fry compared to some! There are people who sell their established blog for millions, and people continuing to earn hundreds of thousands or even millions from their blogs each year, and there are even more people making a very satisfactory living without becoming millionaires – either improving their work-life balance (see number 3 below) or simply earning enough to pay for some of life's goodies.

3. You can opt out of the rat race

We already know that in many industries having a laptop, email and internet connection means you can work from anywhere you please – a café, your hotel room or the kitchen table. But some people are using the internet and their blogs to take this to a new level. Blogging is often international, with readers around the world. So it is not a location dependent occupation and self-styled digital nomads are the new growing breed – hashtags such as #workfromwherever have replaced the cold wet views of British cities for the bamboo and beaches of Bali and Thailand.

Becoming a digital nomad is something many bloggers aspire to and successful blogging is the ideal profession with which to achieve this 'work from wherever' lifestyle. But the best thing is that you are not opting out of the rat race, or giving up on a career, in order to fulfil your ambition. You continue building your career and profile online, while living a lifestyle that those climbing corporate ladders in the real world can only dream of.

Picture this: a digital nomad waking up in a beach hut, doing their 7am yoga on the beach and then conducting their work as usual in their Wi-Fi friendly, sea-facing, low-cost accommodation whilst sipping on fresh coconut water. They school their kids as they go and while many might run travel or lifestyle blogs, others offer consulting, copywriting or web-design services remotely and attract clients through their blogging. If you think it's all hippies, think again. In Ubud in Bali, Hubud is a collaborative working space (think bamboo-constructed building with an organic café and monkeys playing in its gardens) with superfast broadband that hosts 200 local and visiting digital nomads including technology entrepreneurs, remote GPs, fashion designers and photographers.

However, you don't have to aspire to something quite that extreme! You might be a mum who wants to be able to fit work around her children, or you might simply yearn to leave the city for a new life in the country but to still have the opportunities and a position and role in your industry – blogging is a way to ensure that happens. I'd now like to introduce you to the two sisters behind the US-based blog *A Beautiful Mess*. They have brands lining up to work with them, and a diverse range of income streams. Their blog has enabled them to get out of debt and create a lifestyle around their passions, and turned them into a global media brand in their own right.

Sisters Elsie Larson and Emma Chapman from Missouri are the owners of *A Beautiful Mess* (abeautifulmess. com), a DIY crafts and food blog with an income over $1.5 million per year. Elsie and Emma were in debt when they launched in 2010, but now employ five staff and several freelancers. Their blog has around 1.5 million visitors per month. For income, they leverage the blog to sell advertising and have worked with brands including Canon, Adobe, H&M and Valspar. They also sell online courses such as scrapbooking and sewing to their craft audience as well as classes on blogging, Photoshop and Instagram strategy. Plus, they have a range of their own stationery, books, planners, scrapbooking supplies, iPhone covers, cards, art prints and apps – their popular photo editing app has been downloaded more than a million times.

What was the idea behind ABM?

In July of 2007, I (Elsie) started *A Beautiful Mess* as a just-for-fun personal project. In those days, I shared mostly scrapbook pages and personal photos. I didn't know that blogging would ever in a billion years become a side-job, much less my primary career.

Is blogging an industry?

I know it probably bothers some people to call blogging an industry at all, but it is. Blogging is a rapidly evolving form of media. It's a full-time job for thousands of people. It's a legitimate way for companies (from giant corporations to tiny startups) to advertise their goods and services. Blogging is not only a way to kick-start a career, it is a career. A good one! You know what? I believe it hasn't even hit its prime. As an industry, blogging is still just a baby.

→

So is there a career path?

Being a part of a baby industry means you get to lay the groundwork and make your own rules. There are no career guidelines that we have to follow, so it's up to all of us to guide our careers in the direction we'd like them to go. There is tremendous opportunity in blogging. Everyone knows you can make income from advertising, but there is so much more. The branding opportunities, design opportunities, book deals, TV shows, product lines, etc. are endless. If you can dream it, it's probably possible.

You clearly believe in multiple income streams – what is your latest?

Yes, we try to add at least one income stream every year. Some work out well and some don't take, so we tend to launch a few things to experiment. This year (2016) we have already launched our third app, which is its own separate business already. It's called *A Color Story* and it's a filter and photo editing app.

Any advice for new bloggers?

If you go to a blogging conference this year and learn 'everything you need to know', it might all be different by the same time next year. If you take 10 classes by 10 different blogging experts – you might receive a lot of conflicting information. Embrace these changes and contradictions. Keep your mind wide open. There is no one right way to run a blog and there never will be. Change is your friend, don't forget that, and keep your vision alive.

What are you most proud about in your whole journey?

We've learned a lot of lessons the hard way and had many failures too. But, probably the two things I am proudest of are: 1) being able to have a job that I absolutely LOVE and 2) having financial freedom. Elsie and I both know what it's like to be in debt and live pay check to pay check. Happiness has nothing to do with the amount of income you create, but having financial freedom certainly makes life a little easier and gives you more space to create and enjoy all the good things that come your way.

4. You'll get free stuff!

We all like free stuff, right?

Back in my twenties when I worked on a range of glossy magazines, I relished all the freebies that came with the job and the money I saved – I don't think I ever paid for make-up, shampoo, toiletries, hair accessories or gifts for friends. All these, and more, were sent in to the magazines to persuade us to feature them. I even got amazing free holidays – ski trips, spa breaks, flying first class to Mexico and staying on a private island just off Barbados. If you added up the value of all this free stuff, it was like having a several thousand pound salary hike!

Today exactly the same thing is happening but it's not the magazine journalists flying first class any more – it's the bloggers. The media landscape has evolved and brands increasingly recognise the power of bloggers.

A way to boost your professional development

5. You can raise your profile

In today's unstable world, life-long job security is a thing of the past – so every professional person is constantly looking for ways to raise their profile within their industry and be better placed to secure that next position. Whatever you do, developing your personal brand and profile *will* help your business – and that is true whether you run a coffee shop or hair salon, a vet's surgery or doctor's clinic, whether you are a make-up artist, TV presenter, speaker, a celebrity, an actor or a pop star.

Unless you're a faceless organisation, your personal brand and profile has a huge impact on your success and, to be honest, even faceless organisations could benefit from their key people developing personal brands in order to bring more meaning to the organisation – just think about the impact that Steve Jobs' personal brand has on Apple, Richard Branson's has on Virgin and James Dyson's has on Dyson.

Blogging increases your profile – fact. And good blogging adds equity to your professional reputation, which means . . .

6. You can get more opportunity

Raised profile equals more opportunity. You might be the best and most talented in the world at what you do, or the most passionate about a topic, or the most creative when it comes to knitting jumpers from wool straight from the back of a sheep – BUT if no one knows about it then you won't get the opportunities you deserve.

During the book you'll hear me repeating how the default human setting is to wait for opportunities rather than go looking for them. We are such modest creatures and seem to want someone else to point their finger at us and say 'You are amazing!' However, the internet has changed everything by giving us a tool to create opportunities for ourselves. With so many people using it to talk, converse, blog and create and share amazing content, you can't afford *not* to be doing the same – not if you want to create winning opportunities for yourself.

7. You'll learn new online technical skills

This may not leap out of the page as a great incentive, but think about it – how many jobs nowadays require good digital or internet skills? I know for a fact that there are plenty of fantastic potential bloggers who hesitate to do so and quickly become stuck because they feel like technical dinosaurs, unable even to resize a digital photo.

So, even if you just blog as a hobby alongside your day job, you will quickly master all kinds of technical and digital tricks – updating your website, manipulating images, editing video – because it really is *not* difficult. You just need something to motivate you – and who's to say that it won't lead you into some fabulous new job opportunity?

A way to grow your existing real world business

8. You can use blogging to help your existing website

Written blog posts form the majority part of content marketing – and if you're a business owner, you will know that content marketing is the most powerful tool you have and one you can't afford to ignore.

You need to grow your brand and maintain its position in the online marketplace. Blogging can do this – a razor-sharp content strategy including written blogs, video blogs and multimedia content keeps you competitive by driving traffic to your website as part of your sales funnel.

While it takes up some of your time, blogging has another benefit too ...

9. It gives your business a soul and identity

Smartphones, tablets and the internet have opened the door onto what used to be the strictly controlled public face of your business. People now want to see what goes on *behind* the scenes – we are instinctively inquisitive and find it hard to resist peeping into someone's sock drawer! It's the desire to see the real person behind the carefully presented exterior.

So, even if you're the best-presented business in the world, with a revolving glass door at the front and a row of beautiful receptionists to greet clients, you will build *even more* trust by showing a little bit of soul. Post a photo of your team on a night out or celebrating a big sale; or talk about your own story as the business owner, why you started the business and some of the goals you aspire to. In my online press agency, we often used to post behind-the-scenes photos of us standing with the presenters Holly and Phil, having booked one of our clients onto *This Morning*, and all I can say is new clients loved it! After all, our clients *wanted* to go onto *This Morning* to talk about their own situations and here we were showing them that just that week, we'd booked someone else onto the show. Even better, here we were standing with our client and Holly and Phil, inside the *This Morning* studio. Such behind-the-scenes images made it clear to our website visitors that we were the agency to represent them.

The modern world is all about being real and authentic and blogging can help you connect with your customers by showing your human side – and making them smile.

10. It will improve your website's SEO

Content is part of today's outbound marketing – but as a business you still need people to be able to find you online via 'googling', and that means making sure your website ranks high in the search engine lists – a process known as SEO (search engine optimisation) – where it will get much more traffic and create a lot more selling opportunity.

Blogging with carefully selected keywords that people use when typing into the search bar is absolutely essential to good search engine ranking – and using the right keywords has a compound effect. If you keep adding blog posts that fit with these keywords, then not only are you continually adding fresh content for the search engines but with each blog post you add layer upon layer of keywords for the search engines to truly know what your site is about.

The physical size of your website also grows with each blog post, and one of the things Google looks for as a measure of website authority is its size. It's only one of many complex indicators, but a website that is growing by being regularly updated shows that the business is very much alive and kicking.

A way to get more from life

11. You can get (and give) help to solve problems

A lot of people start a blog for personal or cathartic reasons, an online 'diary' where they can creatively vent their daily problems and frustrations. But for some, those problems are more than just minor relationship troubles. Blogging can help you – and it can help other people too.

When John Servante started blogging about his life on *A Diary of a Depressed Student*, he didn't just create an outlet that helped him deal with his own depression – he helped to raise awareness about the stigmas of mental health. Rosie Kilburn on the other hand took to blogging as a way to cope with being diagnosed with liver cancer, using it as a platform through which to sell her range of hand-designed T-shirts promoting cancer survival messages and raising money for cancer charities. A BBC documentary even followed her journey up until she sadly passed away in 2014 aged only nineteen. On her death, her half a million followers flocked to her blog to thank her for her inspiring legacy.

Blogging can be simply all about creating online communities where people in similar situations can help one another, and it just takes one person putting themselves out there to start it.

12. You can change the world

More and more, people are using their voice in the online world to make changes in the real world. The impact that certain blogs have made on global matters is proof that its power should never be underestimated. Even kids can change the world through blogging!

At just nine years old, Hannah Alper launched her blog *Call Me Hannah* to voice her love and concern for animals and the environment. In the three years since then she has organised a Shoreline Clean-up in her community, become a World Wildlife Fund (WWF) Earth Hour Team Captain and travelled across Canada as a featured speaker on the We Create Change Tour.

For nine-year-old Martha Payne, what started out as a school writing project photographing and reviewing her school dinners turned into a food blog that got three million hits and stirred up a storm in her hometown of Lochgilphead in Scotland. With her school under attack in the local papers, Martha, who had been giving each meal a 'food-o-meter' and health rating, was banned from taking photos of her food. But by now her blog had been noticed by celebrity chef Jamie Oliver. Jamie stepped in, the ban was lifted and Martha continued with her campaign for healthier school meals and her efforts to raise money for the charity, Mary's Meals. Donations soared, Martha raised over £130,000 to feed children in Malawi and won a Pride of Britain award.

Let's not forget the adults too. In March 2016, Australian blogger Constance Hall wrote a sincere plea to her audience after a worker at Rafiki Mwema, a charity that creates a safe house for sexually abused young girls in Kenya, reached out to her. On only the first day, Constance received $150,000 worth of donations to the GoFundMe account that she'd set up for the charity – just from people who'd read her post.

So there you are, just a few of the countless inspiring stories of people who really did change the world – simply by blogging . . .

It's an adventure!

13. You genuinely do not know where it will take you

If nothing else, starting a blog can be the first step in an adventure, taking you to extraordinary and completely unexpected places in your life. To illustrate this perfectly, I'd like to introduce you to Andy Weir.

Andy Weir is a former computer programmer who blogged about space and science. He started writing a story on his blog about a manned mission to Mars, which steadily gathered thousands of fans. He turned his blog into an e-book, which was picked up by a publisher and then Hollywood came calling. Yes, you've guessed it, Andy's blog was turned into the Hollywood film *The Martian* (for which Andy was reportedly paid a mid-six figure sum for the film rights).

How and why did you get into Mars?

I've always been a space dork. Mars has fascinated me since I was a little kid. Honestly, I don't remember a time when I wasn't into Mars.

When you first started writing your blog back in 2009, did you think anyone would see it?

I'd spent the previous ten years making webcomics, short stories, fanfiction and other serials and I'd built up a regular readership of about 3000 people by then. So I knew some people would see it, at least. But I had no idea it would become so popular. I only bought andyweirauthor.com after the book came out in print.

What was your big plan?

I didn't have a plan at all. Writing was just my hobby. As the audience grew and people started interacting with the story, it felt awesome. My readers emailed me to correct math or science errors here and there. Even then I didn't know it would get so popular.

So how did you go from no plan to a Hollywood film?

Once the book was done, people started requesting that I make an e-book version so they didn't have to read it in a web browser. So I did and posted it to my site. Then other people emailed saying they wanted to read the e-book, but they aren't technically savvy and don't know how to download a file from the internet and put it on their e-reader. They requested I make a Kindle version they could just get through Amazon. So I did that as well. I set the price at Amazon's minimum allowable price of $0.99. More people bought the book from Amazon than downloaded it for free from my website. That got the attention of Julian Pavia at Crown, a publishing imprint of Random House. He told his colleague David Fugate (a literary agent) about it. David ended up becoming my agent and Julian offered me a book deal. It was a whirlwind of activity because 20th Century Fox optioned the movie rights that same week.

Did you get to be involved in the making of the film at all?

Mostly my job was just to cash the check. Though they did send me the screenplay to get my opinion. In the end, the film is very true to the book, so I'm happy. I got my set payment for the book and that's that. But the film caused a huge spike in sales of the book. I made far more money off those sales than I did from selling the film rights.

→

> **If NASA came up with the first manned trip to Mars and invited you on it, would you go?**
> Nope! I write about brave people. I'm not one of them.

Blogging for 2016 and beyond

From talking to a great many people I know that all that's stopping some from starting their blog is a fear that *'it's all been done already – the internet is full up. Anyway, I'll never be as good as them.'*

Well, it's not! And you can be!

Yes, there are many people – some of them sharing their stories in this book – who started their blog years ago as a hobby or a passion project and slowly realised that they could make some money out of it. Now they're sitting pretty with six figure incomes or they're owners of lucrative online media brands for which advertisers will pay to be featured on and brands will pay for exposure.

Yes, it's easy to look at them and think 'I'm too late'. But you couldn't be more wrong ...

The early bird gets the worm

In any business or industry there are those who were first to the party, who have what is termed 'First Mover Advantage', a competitive advantage that a company earns by being the first to enter a specific market or industry.

Having this head start can certainly bring superior brand recognition and more customers, and it buys time to further develop a product or service while others still haven't noticed what is happening. Of course, if you look at someone who has been running their blog for a few years and has a huge body of content, a library of followers and a huge audience, it's easy to feel overwhelmed.

But there are plenty more worms out there! Let me tell you a few very important things right here by dispelling some common myths ...

Myth #1 – The blogging market is full. No it is not. Because blogging is now an industry, good bloggers will always find rich opportunities. A new wave of opportunity has arisen for new blogging simply because we now know how to make money from blogging – you don't need to blog away for years as a hobby before profiting from it. As Martin Lawrence says in *Bad Boys*, 'this sh*t just got real'. We used to have TV and print media. We now have TV, print media and *online* media. There has never been more opportunity.

Myth #2 – The blogging market will crash. No it won't. We are moving into a period where if you are a person who wants to stand out, get opportunity, make change, you can't afford to not be blogging. If you have a business, you can't afford to not have a website supercharged with a blogging/content strategy. According to consultancy firm McKinsey, nearly three quarters of all luxury goods purchases, even if they take place in physical stores, are influenced by what customers do and see online. McKinsey expect that figure to rise to ninety-nine per cent. A similar study by the Hinge Institute found that the majority of people looking for an expert or service professional turned to the internet to start their search. The same study found that when people are 'checking out' these experts for opportunities, eighty per cent of them visit the person's website. So it's not so much a question of 'why blog', but can you risk *not* blogging?

Myth #3 – Established bloggers will always have the advantage. No they won't. One of the well-known disadvantages of being a first mover is that the early birds bear all the burden, all the economic disadvantage of developing a new market. For the early bloggers of a decade ago that was hours of unpaid time and trial and error, working out exactly how to turn their blog into a business. Now, however, the strategies for successful blogging are well known and well documented as are the different routes to monetisation. You don't need to spend years figuring it out, you just follow a set path. You can learn from the mistakes of the first movers and avoid them, allowing you to advance more quickly. It's not always about doing what everyone else is doing anyway – it's about doing it better or differently. Google is a case in point – they weren't the first in the search market, they just did it better.

So, today's bloggers entering the profession have three distinct advantages over the early birds – the hard work of inventing a new industry has all been done, the digital world that supports and feeds off that industry is continually evolving and the opportunities that can be derived online are still really in their infancy. For the imaginative, resourceful and hard-working blogger, the opportunities have never been greater.

'So how much can I actually make?'

This book talks of the million dollar blogs – and so we'll be meeting many of the world's most successful bloggers to hear their

stories and find out how they did it. We will also be asking experts
in all the complementary fields that support a great blog, such
as content creation and personal branding, to offer their advice.
This means that by the end of the book you will understand the
different threads, philosophies, business models, strands and
opportunities when it comes to creating a million dollar blog.

However, you will *also* be able to see how, if you prefer, your
blog can stay at whatever level brings you the lifestyle that you
dream of – which may be worth a million dollars to you. The
key word here is 'success' – and success means different things
to different people. For some it means cold hard cash – at least
$1,000,000 of it, for others it might mean replacing your existing
income and enabling you to leave a job you don't like, or taking
your life in a new direction, or taking your business to the next
level.

For example, we'll be hearing from people such as Sean Evans,
who founded the independent film review blog *Back to the Movies*.
He is 24 and still lives at home in Stoke-on-Trent but, thanks to
his blog, has a lifestyle that sees him being flown to LA, working
on films and becoming close friends with celebrities.

If you have an illness or a passion, then finding a cure through
blogging or being able to share that passion and make a difference, all from your computer but on a global basis, is priceless.
Likewise, understanding how a system that uses content can
drive leads into your business or make your business stand out is
also invaluable.

So the question is, what is a million dollars to *you*? What do
you hope your blog will bring you in your life? Where do you want
it to take you? Have a think about those questions now, and jot
down your answers in the space provided. The idea is to let your
imagination go wild and think big.

Your blog goalplan

Before you start filling out your plan, allow your mind to expand and think about exactly what you want your blog to be and how it will achieve your ambitions. Now, answer the following questions below.

1. What is the main point of your blog?

_____

_____

_____

2. Does your blog have a greater purpose and mission? If so, what is it?

_____

_____

_____

3. Who are the individuals you'd like to become the biggest fans of your blog? (If you're blogging for a cause, this might be the Prime Minister; if you're blogging to create a media brand, this might be the head of acquisitions at Facebook who might one day buy you out.)

_____

_____

_____

4. What does your dream lifestyle look like and how does your blog fit into that?

_____

_____

_____

5. How hard would you be willing to work if you knew all of
   the above was possible?

   _____

   _____

   _____

   Now, are you ready to get started?

Chapter 2

What is blogging?

We all feel we have a notion of what blogging is, but then again, we probably also have notions of what it is to be an Olympic swimmer, a pop star or a company owner. The truth is, you can never truly understand what a role involves, and all its depths and nuances, until you actually do it. Many bloggers ultimately fail on their journey because they haven't fully grasped what successful blogging is, all its different aspects and the talents required for it. That's why, before you start your own journey, I'd like to give you a fuller idea of what blogging actually is. Wikipedia defines a blog as:

'a discussion or informational site published on the World Wide Web consisting of entries ("posts") typically displayed in reverse chronological order (the most recent post appears first)'.

So, blogging is basically writing stuff and publishing it online. That's all fine, but it doesn't explain the 'why' and the 'what' – *why* do people blog, and *what* do they blog about? I can answer that very simply – they blog about something that matters to them, and they do it to achieve a particular goal . . .

Think of it like this. You're standing in a small room surrounded by closed doors. Each door has a destination on it and the destinations include 'income', 'opportunity', 'respect', 'authority', 'status', 'customers' and 'connection'. Now, most of us strive for one or more of these in our lives and your blog is the key that opens all of these doors – not necessarily at the same time, and not necessarily in the same order, but those doors are there to be opened and your blog and the content you create are the tools that will open all of them for you.

Are bloggers journalists?

Good question! We are living in a strange half way world right now, in which old (or traditional mainstream) media and new media coexist. And this creates tension – most online content is free to access, but traditional news organisations earn revenue by selling their printed content. Some began to create online versions of their publications, charging for access, but while this has been successful for some publications such as *The Times*, others such as the *Sun* have had to make a complete U-turn by offering all of their content for free.

This interface between old and new media fascinates me because of my background in journalism. Until 10 years ago, I was a journalist working on the *Daily Mail*, one of the UK's leading newspapers. I've already outlined how after leaving in 2007, I founded and ran one of the UK's first and leading online press agencies, Talk to the Press (and that is how I discovered blogging for the purposes of growing and positioning a business).

I could see where the scene was moving and knew that the online and content world presented a powerful business opportunity. However, our main clients were the UK's traditional media brands so my position straddled both worlds, →

and I continue to enjoy friendships with many prominent editors and decision makers even today having now sold that business. Being familiar with both worlds, I'm able to see the similarities and the differences.

But does this interface between old and new mean that the blogger is in fact a journalist?

No. For a start, the style of writing is different. As a journalist, you write single articles about single topics, continually moving on to the next topic, and the article is in the voice of the publication you are writing for. As a blogger, you're feeding people's need to keep coming back for more and more on the one topic – and they need to recognise and enjoy your own unique personal voice in all of your own content.

Editors and journalists can be quick to deride bloggers as upstarts and irrelevant. However, I know that there is a vein of doubt coursing through them, eating away at this belief and leaving them scared for their livelihoods and careers, and rightly so. Because the proof is in the pudding (which currently isn't even half baked). Already many huge global new media brands such as *Copy Blogger* and *Mashable* are springing up out of websites that originally started out as 'one man and his blog' (albeit focused on a very specific niche), and plenty of bloggers, as we will be discovering in this book, are living lifestyles and enjoying incomes that most journalists can only dream of.

So – the answer to the question? Well, it's yes and no. Some bloggers, especially those on sites that report news, are definitely journalists, while others are writers, editors, curators, art directors, inspirers, critics, fighters and campaigners.

There is one big difference, however, between a conventional journalist and a blogger. In traditional newsrooms, tasks and responsibilities are divided up between editors, writers, photographers and designers. Bloggers however do everything, the writing, the photography, the layout, the editing, they even often build and maintain their own websites! They also understand how to harness the interactive nature of online media – hence while journalists report to their readers, bloggers interact with them every day.

The best news in all this is for *you*, the person ready right now to become a blogger, and for the future generations of would-be journalists. Once there was just a tiny handful of openings for aspiring journos, and very, very few landed the golden egg where you could write your own column and pretty much say what you liked (within the parameters of the publication). The internet has changed everything. In April 2016, Piers Morgan, whilst speaking at Advertising Week Europe in London, gave print journalism 20 years max and said: 'Too many journalists think it's terrible – get over it! It's the new world – we're not on penny farthings anymore.'

Now anyone and everyone has the chance to define what they want to say and how they want to say it, and to be heard – and some of the best are gaining audiences of a size that most journalists have never had.

Successful bloggers all have one thing in common ...

... they have become *influencers*

The word 'influencer' is huge in the blogosphere, and most bloggers want to be seen as influencers, particularly those who blog to enhance their professional or personal profile (more on this below). This is because ultimately it gives them huge power with the brands and businesses around their niche, and pushes up the rates the blogger can charge as well as bringing more opportunity. Their blog exerts influence over a group of potential purchasers and the blog owners themselves are seen as increasingly important.

Generally, brands face a problem: consumers don't trust their promotional messages and are completely turned off by adverts – and we know that anything produced by or sponsored by a company is basically an advert. Meanwhile, as ad-blocking technology is leading us to a time when we can choose to shut out all online ads, things can only get harder for brands trying to promote themselves.

However, we are very happy to read what impartial people say about products that interest us. From hotel rooms to cars to fashion to home computing, we search out independent reports and recommendations – you only have to look at the runaway success of services like TripAdvisor and reader reviews on Amazon to see that. So an influencer in the blogosphere, able to reach and engage with a brand's target audience, is a very important friend to that brand – and a brand will pay handsomely for this type of access.

Unlike the old celebrity endorsement model, there is room for a *lot* of blogger-influencers, although beyond your own sphere of interest you may remain completely unknown. The blogosphere is divided down by niche, and by niches within niches, so I could be the most powerful fashion influencer with the whole industry at my feet, but over in the digital camera world no one will have heard of me at all. Over there will be a whole other set of influencers related solely to digital cameras.

The fascinating thing about blogger-influencers, is that in the online world, you can have one group of people in the digital camera niche talking about a blogger as though they are the most famous and exciting person on the planet. Yet outside of that niche, there is not a chance anyone will ever hear of them, unless they go delving into that particular topic.

Different brands will look for different influencers, and the same brand might even use different influencers on different campaigns.

Bloggers come in three main flavours . . .

1. those who blog to grow their personal profile,
2. those who blog about their chosen subject/topic and
3. those who blog to enhance their business profile.

Between them, they will ALL produce a varied and diverse mix of content, across platforms. They will most likely have their blog on their website and then also produce unique and exclusive content, including video blogs, for different social media channels.

Before we meet these three types of blogger, I'm going to introduce a concept that you will hear a lot about in this book and in blogging in general: *the niche.*

Every blogger finds their own niche

In the past bloggers tended to start by writing about their own lives and, as a result, would invariably cover all kinds of topics ranging from their frustration with local roadworks to a promotion at work to their holiday in Devon. Now, while that might be fun (or not) for your family and friends to read, and it could serve as a useful portfolio of your writing ability, from a business and money point of view this doesn't make sense.

Why? Because when it comes to any form of monetisation, whether through advertising or selling services, it is hard to see what is being offered or who is being targeted or who the audience might be if the blog content swings from one extreme to another.

Hence the concept of niching – or targeting – your blog by focusing completely on a particular tangible topic or audience where you know there are either people wanting to buy services or products or brands willing to advertise. You then set yourself the goal of reaching that audience or creating an interest in a way mainstream media can't.

We will be discussing how you research and identify niches and their related opportunities in much more detail in Chapter 4, Who Are You and Why Do I Care? – so for now, let's meet these three types of blogger and examine the differences – and the similarities.

Meet the three types of blogger.

1. Being you: blogging to grow your personal profile

Amongst the successful money-making bloggers are those ordinary folk who started as a means of projecting their personalities onto the world and becoming an influencing force. Michelle Phan is one of these, having started blogging about beauty ten years ago.

After two years Michelle increased her personal impact by making a series of 'how to' beauty videos to post on YouTube. Today she has eight million subscribers on the channel and over a billion lifetime views. This has led to a huge array of other ventures, but *all with Michelle at the heart of them*: there is *Ipsy*, her monthly beauty products sampling service that, with more than one million subscribers paying $10 per month, is valued at over $500 million; there is *Icon*, the global lifestyle YouTube channel that she launched in partnership with Endemol; she has her own L'Oréal make-up line named after mother; she's a global spokesperson for Lancôme; and she recently launched *Ipsy Open Studios*, a studio space and online training for beauty industry creators.

Michelle's is a huge success story, but around the world there are thousands of people who have used blogging to create incredible personal profiles that bring in huge opportunity and income.

The first step on this journey is making a choice: the choice to become a highly regarded, well-known influencer in your chosen topic or field. However, the vital part is to make this choice for *yourself*. The American entrepreneur, author and podcaster James Altucher talks about this in his wonderful book *Choose Yourself*. He describes how the world has changed, and *'no longer is someone coming to hire you, to invest in your company, to sign you, to pick you. It's on you to make the most important decision in your life: Choose Yourself.'*

Once you've made this choice, you just use all the wonders of modern technology and communication that are now available to all of us to make your dream a reality.

Now, maybe you think this sounds a little farfetched, more like the stardom dreams of a teenager than a serious business idea? Well, believe me it's not – and it's all thanks to the way the internet has changed and is democratising the world. Now anyone can use blogging to tell the world they are an expert, authority, talent or personality. So, in the past we were programmed to wait for opportunity or recognition to be granted to us – now we can choose to make this happen.

So you've decided it's going to be all about you, but you now have another choice to make – *what will you blog about to enhance your personal profile?* Will you be blogging to entertain, or blogging to become an authority?

Personal profile blogs: Entertainment versus professional authority

Personal profile blogs come in two main guises. Both can bring money, opportunity and fame, but they do so in slightly different ways – by entertaining or leading.

Personal blogging to entertain Entertainment bloggers are effectively publishing their own digital magazine – that features them. They write about their topic or niche, but in a way that makes their own personality an important part of the end-user enjoyment. Their loyal readers come back to the blog to relax, to be shown new things or new products, to laugh, to cry, to look at great images and get new ideas. Entertainment bloggers aim generally at a consumer audience and the route to monetisation will be through adverts, sponsored posts and tie-ups with brands (read more about this in Chapter 3).

Erica Davies, 39, former fashion director of the *Sun* newspaper, is now the proud owner of award-winning fashion blog, *The Edited* (the-edited.com). An excellent example of a successful niche blog which entertains and informs its audience, it is now four years old, has 50,000 visitors a month and is monetised through sponsored posts, affiliate links, retainers with brands and spin-off work including consulting for brands.

Tell us about *The Edited*.

The Edited is my own take on style, shopping and more – and the name is a play on the fact that my background is as a fashion editor. I started blogging generally about clothes and fashion and sharing my posts on my personal Facebook and Twitter feeds.

Tell us about your big turning point.

It was when I introduced 'me' to my blog. As an editor, I'd always been *behind the scenes* at fashion shoots or the hidden influence in the articles I'd write. So when I first began blogging, I didn't initially post images of myself at all. But a few friends suggested I should and so I somewhat reluctantly tried it. I immediately noticed a big difference in traffic and engagement. I was absolutely stunned. I remember thinking 'Who on earth wants to see a 39-year-old mum of two who is not a size 10'. But it turned out quite a lot of people do. I think my readers love the fact that I'm not 19 and that I have a similar figure to theirs but can put together outfits in a way that they might not have thought of.

What's been the most surprising thing for you about blogging?

It's that brands will work with you even if your traffic isn't the highest in your niche. There are tons of blogs with more traffic than me, but my audience is a great fit for the ➜

brands such as high-end high street stores whose clothes I tend to feature. My experience as a fashion blogger is that brands are keen to work with you if you have a beautiful-looking website, an engaged audience, plus an audience that aligns with the demographic they are trying to reach. My audience really listens to me so if I'm focusing on something it will sell – and that is what brands want.

What is your advice for new bloggers?
I think there is a place for everyone, you just have to find your niche and raison d'être. I think mine comes from my history as an editor, people know that I know what I am talking about. At the same time, I don't take things too seriously and I'm ordinary enough for people to really relate to me.

Personal blogging for professional authority Think for just a moment about your industry and chances are you can name the industry figureheads. They are the people who everyone looks up to and admires, whose business seems to be doing the best, and who seem to get the most bookings and charge the highest prices. They are committed and known for their passion. Their opinions are highly respected.

If they're not on mainstream television, they'll have columns in industry publications and speak at industry events instead.

In today's world, this type of positioning doesn't happen by accident or by simply climbing up the career ladder. It can be the result of a deliberate profile and reputation enhancing strategy, for which blogging for professional authority can play a huge role.

Savvy freelancers, service providers and experts do this because they know that huge opportunities come to those who are seen as 'the best'. In my own experience, having previously blogged to grow my business, I now blog for authority in the digital marketing and publicity niche. I am blogging personally but for professional authority.

Now, remember what I said earlier about 'choice'? Your future is your choice, so sitting around waiting for someone else to declare you the leading authority is not the way million dollar bloggers do it! We prefer to let it be undisputedly known that we are the best and we do this by blogging for authority and making our knowledge and expertise absolutely clear. We think of our blogging as building and recording our reputation, one post at a time.

'But who am I to say that I am an authority or expert on this?' Fifty per cent of being the authority comes from stepping up deliberately to take that position, and this means saying credible and authoritative things along the way and displaying genuine expertise. But there is no exam board that subjects all of the world's so-called authorities and experts to measured tests to prove who actually is the definitive authority, we're not in school anymore.

All you are doing is maximising your own opportunity by displaying your knowledge in a way that brings opportunity to your door. You are entitled to do this and in fact you'd be crazy not to. So put those insecurities to one side and get on with it.

'I'm not sure that I WANT to be my industry's leading authority...' That's fine too! No matter what you do, even if you are a freelance plumber or dog walker or hairdresser who wants

more work opportunities, you can still benefit by blogging when it helps communicate as much authority as you need.

American Seth Godin has blogged himself into the position of a global thought leader. He is the author of 18 books such as *Purple Cow*, *Linchpin* and *Tribes* that have been best-sellers around the world and he continues to write daily on his blog (sethgodin.typepad.com) about the marketing of ideas in the digital age, how ideas spread, quitting, leadership and change. His blog is one of the most popular in the world and, in addition to his writing and speaking, he founded the direct marketing company Yoyodyne and the charitable fund-raising platform Squidoo.

When you started, did you have a long-term plan?
The point of blogging, for just about everyone including me, isn't about making a profit with the blog. It's about making a difference. I was one of the earliest bloggers (my email newsletter started in 1991) and from the first day, that's been the goal, that's what I measure.

Did I think it would become one of the most popular blogs in the world? No way. When I saw that a Google search for 'blog' turned up my work in the first five results, I was as amazed as anyone. But yes, all along, the idea was to both share my thinking and to sharpen my thinking as well. If you are disciplined enough to write down a prediction, a way of thinking, a promise, every single day, you can't help but improve yourself. That hasn't changed.

Part of blogging is 'finding your voice' – but people get scared because they don't know what their voice is or sounds like. What are your thoughts on finding a voice?

Write like you talk.

Begin.

Merely begin.

Who should blog?

Everyone who cares should blog.

Anyone who wants to do better.

Or spread an idea.

Or make positive change.

Everyone.

Out of all the things that you do, books, speaking, podcasts, etc., how important is your daily blog to your profile, to reaching an audience and bringing in opportunities?

I'm not going to go down this rabbit hole, because it implies that you can do 'this' to get 'that' and I don't believe it. I think that the speaking gigs and the books happen because of the person behind the blog, not just because I have a blog. The currencies of our economy now are trust and attention. Blogging for attention doesn't work if you haven't earned trust.

Are you ever stuck for ideas and if not, why not?

Nope. Why does anyone get stuck? Write like you talk.

→

What would you say to all those people who enthusiastically start blogs and then give up on them six months later?

It's a little like joining a health club, right?

Don't do it for the destination, do it for the journey.

Is it too late to start a blog?

Oi! Of course it's not too late.

The best time to start was twenty years ago.

The second best time to start is today.

2. Sharing your passion: blogging on a subject/topic

When nineteen-year-old Peter Cashmore sat down one night at his computer in his hometown of Aberdeen and started social media news blog *Mashable*, he could not have expected to become the CEO of a media brand with over twenty million unique visitors a month, revenues of around $40 million and a valuation upwards of $250 million.

Likewise, with *Hypebeast*, what started off as a simple site based on founder Kevin Ma's personal obsession with men's sneakers has become a cult media brand with an e-commerce store attracting an audience of trendsetters and influencers with a staggering twenty-five million monthly page views.

Whatever you are interested in, there is probably an online magazine about it. But many of these online magazines began life as someone's blog where they shared their personal interest in their chosen niche – they didn't start off with the aim of becoming a successful magazine – and the most successful of these represent serious competition to printed magazines too, winning huge audiences and drawing advertisers' money online.

When it comes to starting a blog that could one day become an online magazine or media brand in its own right (and if this thought is in your mind, then I love you for thinking big), it's easy to feel overwhelmed and wonder how you can possibly compete with all the online magazines already out there. But the media landscape is still in huge transition, and the print press continues to hang on too – there is still plenty of opportunity.

However, you must also bear in mind that an online magazine is a much bigger beast than a personal blog. Most online magazines fade and wilt as their owner struggles to keep up with the expectations of their readers in terms of the volume of content, and the expectations of their advertisers in terms of the volume of traffic. That's because many of the successful online magazines post dozens of times *every* day (although they didn't start like that). But the good news is that a magazine has multiple authors, not just one. So as it grows you won't have to write everything yourself (eventually).

Craig Landale, 31, is the owner of *Menswear Style* (menswearstyle.co.uk), a men's fashion blogzine that in 2015 was highly commended in the UK Blog Awards, nominated for 'Best Magazine Website' in the Digital Magazine Awards and nominated in the best Fashion Blog category of the Vuelio Awards.

→

Tell us about how you set up *Menswear Style*.

I was the digital marketing manager for a menswear group, running the blogs and social media platforms for brands such as Suit Direct and Racing Green. On my lunch break I would look at existing men's fashion blogs and see what was happening in the fashion news, purely for inspiration for the content marketing I was doing, and I realised that, compared to what existed for women, there was nothing out there. I saw a major gap in the market and thought it wouldn't be too difficult to set one up and make a name for myself.

How did you build up traffic?

I knew from my background that social media was very important. So I really put a lot of effort into building up Twitter and Facebook, and put a lot of focus into doing competitions to increase reach. The more people liked, shared or retweeted the competitions, the more others heard about the blog. I also had good knowledge of SEO and made sure my website was searchable.

How long did it take you to earn money?

After six months I was quite excited about getting 100 visits a day, which I thought was amazing but of course is very low compared to the traffic I get today, and with traffic going up each week I started looking at monetisation. Today, you probably couldn't earn money with such a small number of visitors per day, but you could certainly start to get free products to review.

Even to this day, one of my strategies is to think of as many different income streams as possible. I do affiliate marketing, banner advertising, have an affiliate-based shop and I also do sponsored posts. We now also have apps and an e-book entitled *ABC of MAN*. Our lifestyle chapter has developed hugely as the blog has expanded and now includes sub chapters such as Tech, Food & Drink, Travel, Health & Fitness and Cars, all of which bring in new opportunities and markets for monetisation.

What is your advice for talking to brands?

Because I'd been a digital brand manager, I was used to people calling me and trying to get our company to pay them for sponsored posts. So I knew what digital marketing managers wanted to hear and I knew the boundaries. If they said to me: 'budgets are tight', I would suggest that I did something for free in order to begin building a relationship. Then I'd contact them again in April at their budget-setting time and by then, of course, we had the relationship.

How busy is the site now?

I get 5000 hits per day and the majority comes from Google search. We've published over 5000 articles in total and I have two photographers, six writers and ten contributors producing content for the site.

→

How do you decide what to post?

A lot of the articles are 'how tos', based on things that people are searching for. One of our most popular articles at the moment is 'hairstyle trends for 2016'. I would say I base the posts 50 per cent on what is current and happening in men's fashion and 50 per cent on keyword research which tells me what people are looking for. I strategically try to answer popular menswear questions – how to wear a cravat, how to fold a pocket square, etc. I look to Google keyword and the Google trends tool, and I look to Google autocomplete for inspiration.

How has the blog changed your life?

I'm doing something I really love, I get sent lots of free clothes, I've got a great income, cash in the bank and I've just bought a house in London – I'm really happy.

What is the most exciting thing for you about the blogosphere for 2016?

There's a new generation of teenagers that no longer have to approach McDonald's for their first paid job. Instead they realise 'I can just use my computer in my bedroom!' For the first time ever, people understand this as a job that can be very flexible and let them do something they truly enjoy. The same goes for those who are already trapped in jobs they don't like. They don't have to be trapped anymore.

3. Growing your business: blogging for business profile

Whenever people talk about blogging for the profile of a business their language changes, their tone drops, they put on their serious face and they suddenly start talking about *content strategies*.

But let's be clear about a few things – ALL blogging is a content strategy, ALL effective content strategies involve blogging – and a content strategy is part of a bigger business marketing strategy which is about growing the business, improving its visibility and getting more leads. The only difference between business blogging and the other two types is that instead of building an audience that will appeal to brands or a consumer audience that you can help brands sell things to, your focus is on attracting an audience who might need whatever it is your business sells. Your audience is people who might become your customers.

It's all to do with education and persuasion

Your business blog helps to communicate your authority and expertise, and educate your audience about what you specialise in.

Emma Jones MBE is the founder of *Enterprise Nation* (enterprisenation.com), which supports and guides small business owners through advice, tools, events and campaigning. Since launching in 2005, *Enterprise Nation* has supported tens of thousands of entrepreneurs and →

content is at the heart of the organisation's success, both in terms of starting the business initially and continuing to power its growth today.

How did *Enterprise Nation* grow to what it is today?

When I first launched *Enterprise Nation* back in 2005, all we had was our blog and I was the only person blogging. The blog enabled me to publish a number of books and grow our reach and I hired a part-time blogger. Now, we have three people working full time on content and the range of our content has increased over the past ten years to suit the needs of how consumers want to consume content. As well as the blog, we publish content on YouTube, podcasts on iTunes and via webinars – but the blog is at the heart of all our content.

Did you have a specific content strategy?

Yes, I follow the philosophy of the three 'c's' of content, community and commerce. That involves building content around a specific topic (in our case, small businesses), a community of people then forms around that content, which they have done, and then we would turn that into a business and commercialise that community. We wanted to build trust and credibility with small businesses and then turn it into a viable commercial opportunity. Now, small businesses pay us for membership to come to events and we have a good stream of income from big commercial sponsors.

So you used content to start, does it still matter now?

If we stopped producing content, we'd stop having an opinion, we'd lose traffic and we'd lose our reason for being. Content is the beating heart of the company and without it, all the rest of our business activities would stop. We publish at least once a day, but during periods when there is a lot going on for small business owners, we publish up to four times a day.

What does the content give *Enterprise Nation*?

It's partly about traffic. Our content shared on social media gets people coming to the site to see what we are about. It's also about credibility: writing about small business owners and the issues they face every day gives us the credibility to be the voice of small business.

Should all business owners be blogging?

Whether you are selling accounting software or flowers, content gives you an ability to have an opinion and become an expert in your field. When you look at consumers buying things, even flowers, they want to go to someone who knows what they are talking about. That is even more the case when someone is buying accounting services or business services: they want to know that the person from whom they are buying has the expertise to deliver. Content is a brilliant way to show off that expertise.

If you have any doubt at all about whether it's worth blogging and pursuing a content strategy, just ask *Elegant Themes*, a technology company that produces Divi, a web builder popular with web designers ...

In a recent newsletter, *Elegant Themes* detailed the outcome of their 2015 content (aka blogging) strategy, and the results are both astounding and staggering. They reveal they have a daily content creation strategy and post every single day of the year.

Their posts contain anything that might be useful to their target audience (web designers) from dealing with client contracts to how to improve e-commerce sites and, of course, they also publish posts that promote their own products (namely their Divi site builder).

When talking about their content strategy, they said: 'In 2015 we published 365 posts, approved 19,335 comments, and saw 12.8 million blog page views. Our total post count rose to 919 published posts, our total comments rose to 58,304 approved comments, and our total page views rose to a whopping 27.8 million blog page views.'

Now, no successful business wastes a single penny on ineffective marketing, so clearly this works for them. Of course it does – imagine if 27.8 million people viewed *your* web pages and 58,304 people commented on what *you* had to say or sell!

CAUTION: business blogging is a serious matter!

A business content strategy is far too important and specialised to be delegated to the bosses' over-worked PA. If you do not have the time or skills to create your blog yourself you may have to outsource it to a professional content writer.

But whatever way you invest in your content, a return on that investment does not come overnight. *All of the business blogs we will hear from* committed to a long-term and consistent content strategy, and put huge amounts of thought and creativity into producing engaging, useful blog posts.

So where to start?

Put in its simplest terms, this involves you setting up a website, sitting down, starting typing and pressing publish.

You also set up a social media profile and you share out your posts. You phone your mum and tell her to visit your website right now and read your post. You might film a video of you talking about this (a vlog). Then you think of the next thing that you'd like to write about in your field and you write it, and you repeat this process over and over again.

BUT hold your horses! BEFORE YOU DO THAT, remember I don't want you to start until you understand the big picture of blogging and how all these different puzzle pieces come together to form a million dollar blog. We're only just getting started. You've just learned about the different types of blogs so in your mind you might have an idea of the type of blog you want to set up, or a clear vision for the blog you are already running, which will help you move forward on your blogging journey. But there is more to learn yet.

We're going to look now at two further elements of successful blogs: understanding your niche and developing your personal brand. Then we're going to examine all the various ways that blogs today, in 2016 and beyond, can earn YOU money – serious money. This can then be the necessary motivation at the back (or front!) of your mind as you work through the rest of the book and prepare to launch your very own blog.

Chapter 3

Who are you and why do I care?

Whatever your reason for blogging, understanding your own niche is essential. Take Perez Hilton, self-acclaimed as 'the internet's most notorious gossip columnist' and one of the world's most high-profile bloggers. Perez uses his blog to break 'hot celebrity news' from Hollywood, much of it derived from attending its regular star-studded events.

Love it or loathe it, his blog gets twelve million readers a month and has turned Perez into a celebrity in his own right and allowed him to launch his own radio show, appear regularly on television and in the press, and expand his empire with a series of further websites including fashion website CocoPerez.

Now, if Perez suddenly went off piste on his blog and started writing about mainstream news, politics or skiing, his readers would become confused – the brand and identity that 'is' Perez would be diluted. Instead his success comes as much from never veering away from his personal niche as it does from the blog itself – he understands his audience and consistently delivers.

He's not alone. The biggest blog stars become known for their very clear positioning and their names become synonymous with the niche they serve. 'Niche' is one of the biggest buzzwords in the blogosphere and all bloggers need to work out who they are, what they offer and what their niche is going to be.

Your niche is your focus, your premise, your raison d'être. It is, in part, the particular topic or cause that your content is focused around – but, as we will see shortly, it's also more than this, it's *you* as well. Whether your role is as writer, editor or curator, the niche you are serving must always remain paramount in your thoughts.

Niches go deeper than topic

'I see – well that's easy; my niche is fashion/dogs/travel/cooking . . .'

No, that's not a niche – that's a topic.

Imagine you are selling lawn seed – your topic is gardening, but your niche is lawn care. Traditional media was identifiable by topic – for example, gardening – but *within* that topic are dozens of specialist niches, including lawn care. Thanks to the internet, this is the experience that consumers now expect, the ability to drill down and find exactly the mini-topic that interests them most – that's the level at which you pitch your unique blog.

But even a specialist sub-topic isn't enough to make your blog unique . . .

Your niche is more than just your focused area of interest – your blog is also *you*, presenting your own unique point of view and particular expertise. There are plenty of bloggers and online magazines covering Hollywood, but Perez imbues his blog with his personality, the glimpses into his world, his own sense of humour, his face, his own life and story and most importantly his own unique spin on things. Other bloggers can't directly compete with that simply because they can't be him. We'll be finding out more about who you are in the next chapter.

Your niche includes your readers too

Take two food bloggers in the 'clean eating' space (currently huge in the online world and extremely popular and competitive). One, a twenty-something blogger, attracts and gains an audience that is young, carefree, childless and in the early stages of their career. Another, who has children herself, attracts an older audience of mums. Although essentially very similar in their niche, each blog will have different opportunities for monetisation. The twenty-something blogger may attract younger hipper brands and opportunities on YouTube, whereas the family blogger will most likely attract more traditional household brands looking to reach her more mature audience, along with more conventional 'off site' opportunities such as book deals.

So, two bloggers can effectively be blogging about the same sorts of things but attracting different audiences.

Before we forget that a successful blog doesn't have to be in a lifestyle or household niche, let me share with you the story of Paul Staines, one of the UK's most successful and high profile bloggers, and how following his passion – a strong belief that governments are shifty – and excelling at Westminster-oriented content has allowed him to carve out an incredibly defined and lucrative niche where his audience is known to include the Prime Minister and all those in power in Westminster. You can even hear his unique personality shine through my interview with him!

Paul Staines, 49, is the creator and owner of the political blog *Guido Fawkes* (an old form of the more familiar name Guy Fawkes) seen at order-order. com. The blog is written from the perspective of Fawkes, 'the only man to enter Parliament with honest intentions (to blow it up with gunpowder)'. Staines is the first blogger to 'take the scalp' of a serving British minister following the resignation of Peter Hain in 2008. He also exposed John Prescott's extramarital affair and his exposé of leaked emails, proposing a smear campaign targeting top Tories, led to the resignation of Damian McBride and the 'smeargate' scandal. He is consistently named as one of the most powerful men in the UK.

How did you get started?

Before blogging, I'd been working in bond broking but in 2001 I went through two years of litigation and in the end had to declare myself bankrupt. Meanwhile people were starting to blog and write about things like the Gulf War, but it was in the form of very long articles of 2000 words plus. I thought 'I want to do this', driven by my strong feeling that we had a pretty crappy government and a shabby opposition.

So I started writing articles for other blogs, but mine were short and snappy and, with everyone else writing 2000 word essays, no one would publish them. Then one blog owner asked why I didn't set up my own blog, and I remember saying to my wife 'I'm going to into blogging' – she had thought I would be going back into bond

➔

broking and wasn't impressed, particularly when, after putting Google ads on the site, I still only earned enough to cover the mobile phone bill.

How did you figure out the monetisation?

I didn't really make any money until 2008 when, mainly to placate my wife, I set up my advertising agency called MessageSpace. At that time a few political blogs including *Guido Fawkes* were really gaining traction and I sat one day with a group of other blog owners in a hotel lobby and we realised that what we needed was a corporate vehicle to sell ads on our behalf. So two of us decided to set one up and, while continuing to write our blogs, we literally cold-called advertisers to get it all going. Now MessageSpace is a multi-million-pound business that sells advertising space across twenty-five political websites and blogs.

What about *Guido*?

Back then in 2008, I was pricing adverts on *Guido* at £500 but not having much success selling them. Then it became clear to me that I wasn't thinking about it quite right. Someone said to me 'Do you know the PM reads your blog?' and a lightbulb went on. We started pricing them at upwards of £10,000 and suddenly they sold. You see, monetising is all about knowing your audience. I have 100,000 readers per day on *Guido*, but the ads aren't aimed at most readers, the people my advertisers want to reach are the 5 per cent of my readers who are running the country – and they know that costs money.

How does *Guido* make money?

We sell stories to newspapers but are mainly advertising-funded via revenue from MessageSpace. We have got the most traffic of all the political blogs as we are more mid-market and the most entertaining – and we write great headlines. I would describe our product as being tabloid but with a knowing edge.

Our readers are often on the blog ten times a day. If you go around a newsroom, you will see that the entire political desk has *Guido* constantly open on a browser tab. It's no secret too that Tory MPs are addicted to *Guido*. Every morning they get a daily summary email telling them what all the day's media is saying and *Guido*'s stories are second on that list.

What have you learned about politicians?

They have a need to be loved, especially before an election. Before elections, the phone never stops ringing because my blog has influence. Afterwards, they won't take our calls.

You've become famous for taking out MPs, was that intentional?

I always say if we don't take out one MP a year, we get bored. During my 20s I had a suspicion that it's really hard to get to the top of politics without compromising yourself almost to the point of corruption. You start out as an idealist, but then you compromise here, sort out a donor there, a union over there and the next thing you know you are Tony Blair. However, the traditional media are too

→

close and often end up protecting their client politicians. So I saw my role as making sure politicians feel worried that we will find out. I feel even more cynical about the whole thing today and none of my original suspicions have turned out to be unfounded.

Do you monitor site traffic?

Yes! I used to laugh at the rumours that Nick Denton who founded Gawker Media shouted at his team if they didn't get enough traffic but now I'm just as bad. There's hell to pay if we don't have 100,000 hits a day. OK, so that's a bit of an exaggeration, but I do send out an email every day about who had the most popular stories. We probably publish around 15 stories a day, sometimes 20. We generate stories based on news flow (i.e. what politicians are actually out doing and saying) – some come in via tip-offs and I also encourage my team to go out drinking with people inside Westminster, that's often the best way to get a story.

You're consistently ranked as one of the most powerful men in Britain. What do you say about that?

All I care about is that I rank higher than the BBC's Nick Robinson.

Getting started on your niche

So how do you choose between niches? How do you decide on a niche and make it your own? The best place to start is with . . .

The four fundamental pillars of niche

Pillar #1: Who are *you*?

This question covers both your interests – what motivates you and what you know about.

So, what are *you* all about? What are you interested in, what are you passionate about? What do you talk about most often? What do you do in your spare time? What things do you enjoy buying and get really excited about? If money was no object, how would you spend your time? Start writing down your thoughts in a notebook.

The most respected bloggers often tend to be experts in their field. I don't mean conventional experts such as doctors and lawyers who studied the subject at university and have a degree in it – although of course you can be one of those and it's great if you are. I am talking about something you are genuinely good at. Don't forget, everything is different in this new online world. Bloggers are making millions out of topics, such as crafting, that don't come with university degrees. So ask yourself, what do people talk to you about and ask for your advice on?

Maybe you're not *yet* an expert? Don't panic. It's perfectly possible to be perceived as a different type of expert with a blog that is more of an exploration or learning curve than a definitive statement by an establishment expert. Many bloggers don't claim to be experts, but instead state clearly that they are interested in a topic and how it works, and their blog is charting their own learning experience. A friend of mine has become, by way of a blog, a 'self-help' expert through charting her journey of reading and applying the wisdom offered in self-help books to her own life. Obviously, along the way, she learned a lot about the theories of self-help too. Readers love this as they feel they are connecting with someone on their own level and going along for the genuine journey rather than being preached at by someone who thinks they know it all. We'll be finding out a lot more about who you are in Chapter 6.

Pillar #2: Where does who you are meet a popular topic or need?

It takes all sorts to make the world go round and technically there is room for everything and more on the internet. But if you are starting blogging with business in mind rather than just as a passion project, you need to marry up what you have just learned about yourself (the characteristics that will help you become a productive blogger) with what others are genuinely interested in. If you're thinking of business blogging (whether as a business in itself or as a way to drive leads for your own business, consultancy or freelance work), you're going to need a market for what you are writing about.

Paul Staines' story, above, is a case in point. Politics clearly has a massive following and Paul had always been interested in and passionate about politics. But his blog works so well because of the combination of topic – politics – and his personal take on it – that 'governments are crappy'. When something happens in the political world, he immediately has a strong opinion. He feels angry about certain areas of politics. This personal passion aligns perfectly with the hunger that political observers have for someone to 'pop the balloon' and say it how it is. That is his niche, not the topic of politics but his unique marriage of topic, style, personality and clearly defined audience.

Pillar #3: Who do you want to reach?

This is about your audience. Who are you trying to reach and con-nect with? What are they looking for? How can you create content that engages them? Let's think again about Paul Staines and how he has cultivated an audience that includes the Prime Minister, and then just how powerful his blog has become because of the fact these huge power players are in his audience. It is the same with Mummy bloggers, who we will be hearing a lot more about shortly.

When it comes to who you are reaching, there are three words you'll hear again and again: audience, community, tribe. The question you might have is what is the difference between them? Just like any business, bloggers have a customer base and in this case, broadly speaking, this base is your readers or audience. There are certain words that are thrown around the blogosphere that further categorise this following, but what exactly do they mean?

It doesn't matter what your niche is, if you have a blog, you have an **audience**, even if that audience is just one person! An audience tends to be a one-way following that passively watches or reads.

A **community** on the other hand is a two-way conversation. It is a living, breathing thing that is interactive and social. Communities are essentially 'gathering places' for members who share some of your worldviews and interests and in the case of a blogger, your community may gather on your blog and comment on your posts, or they may gather on a different social platform, such as Facebook, on your page, or most commonly in a group you might have set up that complements your blog, where you have two-way conversations with them. So people in your com-munity engage with you, hear you and like you – but they are not necessarily totally nuts about you, not when it comes to spreading your story.

That's where **tribes** come in. The thing that tribes have above all else is passion for you and your brand. In every niche are bloggers with their own tribes who live and breathe your content; they purchase your services and products; they promote your brand across all their social media channels. In the traditional world, your tribe, were you a musician, would count as those diehard fans who come to every concert and camp outside your hotel room. They are your biggest fans and assets – and therefore what all bloggers should strive for because those in your tribe promote you, as Jadah Sellner, the co-founder of the million dollar blog *Simple Green Smoothies* tells us.

Jadah Sellner is the co-founder of *Simple Green Smoothies* (simplegreensmoothies.com), a website, blog and community that has helped over a million people through their 30-day Green Smoothie Challenge and has close to a million dollars in annual revenue through books and digital products. Their blog and social media content revolves around recipes, inspiration and uplifting messages. Jadah also mentors business owners on building communities and businesses led by love.

You often speak about community and tribes and their importance, tell us more.
To build a community and tribe around what you do, you have to think of yourself as a lighthouse: you are the light and people are attracted to you. But you can't just be broadcasting anymore – you have to then go out and

interact with people, which is why communities are usually on the social platforms belonging to a business or blog.

What are the benefits of tribes and community?

If you can tap into the power of community building and attract a tribe, you will stand out in your industry as a leader. Your community and especially your tribe love what you are about and your movement, idea, product or service spreads faster. The *Simple Green Smoothies* community is spread across social networks and our site, we have 400,000-plus followers on Instagram, 300,000 fans on Facebook and 350,000 email subscribers to our newsletter. Community is so important to us – we even have a team of community happiness specialists who help us interact and respond to people.

Simple Green Smoothies is such a success story, but where did you start?

We all start at zero. In 2012, we had zero followers, zero email subscribers, zero team and zero money. My business partner Jen and I were running a parenting blog called *familysponge.com* and we thought that would be our million dollar business. Prior to that, I'd run a bricks and mortar nursery and I'd thought that would be my million dollar business! *Simple Green Smoothies* came about while coming up with e-book ideas for the parenting blog. I'd lost 27lbs after drinking one green smoothie a day for a month and so we decided to launch an e-book called *Simple Green Smoothies*. I started an Instagram account called *Simple Green Smoothies* to promote

→

the e-book ahead of its launch. It grew really quickly from zero to 30,000 and we realised people would be really confused if we sold a green smoothie book from a parenting blog – and that's where the *Simple Green Smoothies* site was born.

How did you build your social media following so fast?

Firstly, we chose a social platform where our audience are hanging out, but also where we could shine and were excited to be. That is because people can feel if you are not all in and don't love what you do. For us, that was Instagram. Then there are three things that work really well – no matter what social media platform you are on. Firstly, posting valuable content, right there in the platform. A lot of bloggers say go to this link and try to get people to their blog, but I really believe you need to provide the valuable content where people are. They will go to your site once they have had a chance to get to know, like and trust you. Secondly, is engaging with influencers and seeing if they will share your content. Consider it micro guest posting. I went to a live boot camp and made smoothies for the boot camp instructor. She gave us a shout-out and we went from 800 to 3000 followers. Always look for people who can give you shout-outs and add value to them. The third is engagement. We posted recipes on Instagram two to three times a week. I spent the rest of my time searching hashtags and interacting with people who looked like they would like green smoothies. It's not just about putting out noise. It's about interacting with real human beings.

What's your advice to new bloggers?

To be innovative. When we started in 2011, we looked at everyone who'd started in 2008 and wondered if we were too late. People starting now might feel the same way. The opportunities are always there and marketing principles are the same – it's just the business model shifts over time. We had an e-book that made us a million dollars in sales in two years. Now we see huge opportunities in digital products. A big thing that I really believe in is getting an accountability partner – someone who is at a similar phase in the journey to you. Someone to cheer you on when you are feeling down and out.

Pillar #4: What is the competition doing – and *not* doing?

Competition is good! If you're starting blogging now or upping the ante with your existing blog, you're highly likely to have competition – and that's great because it means there is demand, a market and an audience to be found in your niche. Doing an analysis of the competition will also show you how the niche is monetised. What are other people doing? Where are they earning their money – on site through affiliate links, sponsored posts, e-commerce and banner ads, or off site through speaking opportunities, consulting and book deals?

However, you *then* need to differentiate your blog from theirs – remember, this is all part of defining your niche. So ask yourself the three 'Whats': 1) What can I learn from them? 2) What can I do differently from them? and 3) What are they *not* doing?

Of course it's possible that the basic business principles of supply and demand will come into play. Some niches may simply be full or overcrowded and difficult to gain traction in, but that doesn't mean you should forget about them. One way to stand out in a crowded niche is through a powerful personal brand (which we will be talking about in the next chapter). Another way is to think of a way to do things differently – perhaps you can break down the niche into a further sub-topic, or present your content in a different way, there are always gaps in a market.

Paul Johnson's story shows how important it is to define your own section of a topic or even a niche, and then to make it indisputably your own through your style and content.

Paul Johnson, 44, is the owner of *A Luxury Travel Blog* (aluxurytravelblog.com), one of the world's leading luxury travel blogs with over 150,000 monthly visitors and over a million followers on social media. Although there are thousands of travel bloggers, Paul's blog is listed #1 in the Rise Global list of the top 1000-plus travel blogs. He also recently scooped the 'Top Travel Influencer' award from *WIRED* magazine, as well as 'Best Travel Blog' in the Travelmole Web Awards. *A Luxury Travel Blog* has been named as one of the best travel blogs in the world by the *Daily Telegraph* and the 'best for luxury'. Paul also enjoys brand partnerships with a number of large companies including the likes of American Express, Bentley, Land Rover and Panasonic.

How does defining your niche help you?

The brands I work with know that through my site they can reach a very particular audience. This means that I don't just work with luxury *travel* brands, luxury brands in general know that by partnering with me they can reach a large number of targeted individuals who are adventurous and enjoy high disposable income.

How did you get started?

Before starting *A Luxury Travel Blog* I ran a web design agency that specialised in websites for the tourist industry. We later evolved into making travel websites in-house and generated commissions through affiliate marketing. That was successful: at one stage we were the biggest seller of rooms for Premier Inn in the UK. Alongside this I started *A Luxury Travel Blog* as a hobby – something I'd dabble with during my lunch hour. But around 2012 Google's algorithm changed and our booking sites which had ranked well were affected. That's what gave me the push to go full time with the blog.

How is the blog monetised?

Mainly through sponsored posts and banner advertising. I've worked with brands such as American Express, Bentley, Land Rover and Panasonic. Working with top level brands brings other benefits including new content. For example, Land Rover ran an expedition to mark the launch of a new Range Rover for which they drove three prototype vehicles from Solihull to Mumbai over 50 days. They paid me to join them on their leg from Kathmandu to Delhi over 10 days,

→

which was great in itself. But the journey provided material for multiple posts on the blog and social media.

You've cornered the luxury travel niche – how have you done it?

Through a lot of hard work developing quality content – and plenty of it. In the early days the blog was written exclusively by me. Today, I have over 400 contributors, with 50–60 of them writing for the site each month. This allows us to publish more volume than most – up to 100 posts per month – without compromising on quality. This provides us with more material to share on our social channels which are well developed because we've been around from the start. The site is also simple to use – visitors can scan it easily and find what they are looking for, its design has changed very little in seven years, my priority is always the content.

Are you happy with the traffic you get?

I'm never happy with my traffic levels. Even when it gets to 500,000 visitors, I know it can always do better. To me, the marketing of the website is a job that is never finished. My mind set is that you can always pull in more visitors. I always work on getting more traffic but I also look at the type of traffic, such as general searches *vs* social media. With social media you get the people that stumble upon something and are curious to have a look but they tend to leave the site again fairly swiftly. By contrast someone who has gone to Google and specifically entered 'best restaurants in New York' has set out to do that. These searchers are more engaged, and that's what the brands like about my blog.

What about your income?

I earn a good living from the blog and it gives myself and my family some incredible opportunities – I travel solo on trips taken during term-time but combine my work with family trips during the school holidays. In the past year we've been to Dubai and on to the Maldives. We have been on safari in Africa. We've even stayed in the ultra-grand Badrutt's Palace hotel in St Moritz in Switzerland – it is so upscale that just off from the lobby is a Raphael worth millions hanging on the wall.

Mummy blogging

So far we've shone the spotlight on three of the most popular groups of blogging niches – fashion, beauty and lifestyle – but I don't want to go any further without mentioning one of the biggest (and most crowded) highly visible life-related niches – the so-called 'Mummy blog'.

Mummy bloggers might be derided by some, but you are about to see the power of a clear niche in terms of the subject and the audience. Having first appeared in the early 2000s, parenting blogs have grown phenomenally ever since. Little surprise, since the Mummy blog is a perfect example of how technology can facilitate the next evolution of something that already exists – in this case, people simply recording and sharing their experiences.

A few generations ago, every mother would have been given or bought a baby book following their birth of a child and used it to diligently capture milestones and store photographs and mementos. It was a rare visitor to the home who escaped without first being persuaded to 'enjoy' them! Since then, as we've increasingly lived our lives online, this behaviour has followed effortlessly to create the Mummy blog.

But where's the glamour in nappies?

You'd be surprised! And certainly, some Mummy bloggers have earned remarkable status – *and* the valuable trappings that come with it. But while most don't have the same celebrity status as some of the lifestyle and beauty/fashion bloggers, writing about which brand of baby powder will generate the fewest nappy rashes has turned these Mummy bloggers into a force to be reckoned with.

Brands know women listen to other people, which means Mummy bloggers ARE taken seriously and can run viable businesses being bloggers, which in turn attracts more women to do the same thing.

These are real mothers sharing real stories about the trials and tribulations of parenthood and as their audience is made up of other mothers or mothers to be, it is massive and will never diminish – and with a massive audience come massive rewards.

> Vicki Psarias is often cited as one of the UK's most successful Mummy bloggers. She is a multi-award-winning screenwriter and director who, following a TV and film career making drama, documentaries and music videos, began her parenting and lifestyle blog

Honest Mum (honestmum.com) which covers family life, food, fashion, beauty and film. Her site gets 80,000-plus visitors a month and she has collaborated with brands including Selfridges, Harrods, Ralph Lauren, John Lewis, Very, Waitrose, Evian, H&M and many more.

Tell us about how and when you got into blogging.

I started in November 2010, at which point I had a 10-month-old child. I'd suddenly gone from being a busy, successful director to maternity leave with a baby. I was suffering from a traumatic birth and was frankly feeling lonely and scared.

I'd entered a strange new world that felt totally foreign to me too and if I'm honest, I found life was pretty boring and relentless (no one tells you how boring life with a baby can be). I would recount stories of Babydom to a great filmmaker friend of mine and she convinced me to write about it. Within just two weeks, advertisers had contacted me to work with them and within four, my blog was a finalist at the BritMum's Brilliance in Blogging Awards in the Fresh Voice category. The latter really helped me feel confident about my voice again.

How has Mummy blogging changed since then?

In 2010, parenting blogs in the UK were just starting up (I was one of the first here) – following the US parenting bloggers' lead. We bloggers have and are constantly meeting in others a need for an honest and, thus far, alternative view of parenting to that of the mainstream media. Parenting blogs help others feel far less

→

alone and far more normal and have the power to inform, support and inspire others. From a work-wise perspective, we are hugely respected. I'm asked to attend fashion weeks in London and Paris, and feature as an expert in my field in the press and on TV. We parenting bloggers are being paid to wear the brands we work with, push the prams and go on holidays. We are walking, talking, living digital influencers and are a new and diverse talent pool brands need and love to work with.

What do you like most about blogging?
It has been life changing for me. I used to work 12–15 hours a day on set and when I had my first child, I returned to directing when he was one. Now my site means I still work full time but I choose my *own* hours; I have Fridays off with my youngest and if my kids are ill, I'm around. I have a flexibility that would have been impossible before and I get to earn a great living doing something creative I love.

What I personally adore about my blogging career is that I can be a director, a writer, a vlogger, a presenter, a consultant and an entrepreneur on any given day. I can't think of any other career which offers that diversity! In terms of our lifestyle, it's been just wonderful. I can offer my children luxury holidays thanks to my job and I get to share my passions with the world. I also love featuring in and writing for glossy magazines and presenting on TV –working with ITV and SKY News have been dreams come true.

How does blogging compare to being a filmmaker?

When I was a filmmaker, if I put in 100 per cent I'd only ever get 50 per cent back. With blogging, I put in 100 per cent and get a million back (sadly not bucks – yet)! It doesn't make mathematical sense but that's what happens. When I write something on beauty, for example, I have global beauty brands approaching me asking, 'Can we put you in a film? Can we pay you to front or promote this campaign?' It's an encouraging, fulfilling way to work as a creative.

What have been the highlights so far?

What matters the most to me, above everything, is the emotional connection I have with my readers, the way you can move or transform how others think of themselves for the better, in an instant.

I shared a photo of myself in a red bikini in Jamaica last year that went viral. It was captioned with me saying it was the first time in two years I had felt confident in a bikini despite some stretch marks on my tummy. Thousands upon thousands of women commented and emailed saying they were now going to wear a bikini again, too, and take their children swimming. Just the other day I had someone attend a workshop and say she discovered my work through that photo. It truly showed me the power of blogging. I then started a campaign off the back of the shot titled 'Proud in My Bikini' encouraging others to share their own pictures on social media and their blogs too.

→

What advice would you give to anyone wanting to break into the industry?

Anyone can start blogging but if you were to look at me and think I've got it all nailed, 100 per cent of the time, then I haven't! It's the most dynamic, ever-changing platform. You just need to hone your voice, work at connecting with readers on social platforms, write what you yourself want to read – and simply GO FOR IT.

The particularly potent power of Mummy bloggers

It's said that behind every great man is a great woman. Studies show that women make 95 per cent of the purchasing decisions in a household, proving that in today's society the woman is the head of the household – she holds the purse-strings, she is the decision maker and she is the ultimate authority. This makes Mummy bloggers some of the most influential people on the internet, with their impact going via their online audiences into the very hearts of households across the country.

So Mummy bloggers are more than just a particular group blogging in a particular niche. They are a direct conduit for brands to the people who control the household money and make the key spending decisions – women. Even better, those mothers who are digital influencers online are also powerful influencers offline, typically in their communities and amongst their mummy friends.

How many Mummy bloggers are there?

It's impossible to get an accurate figure, but to illustrate the scale of this niche there are 8000 parenting bloggers on the Mumsnet Bloggers Network alone, a platform that brings together the best of bloggers content from across the web onto one website and then promotes that content to the vast Mumsnet audience.

In fact, if you're a woman of childbearing age the chances are you know at least one person who has tried or wants to do Mummy blogging. Part of its success and appeal is that it fits so well when women's lives are suddenly filled with the sound of little feet. If they are at home with small children, they can work on a quick blog post in the way they couldn't fit in other 'work'. Many Mummy bloggers aren't trying to make a business out of it but are simply using it as an online diary of their family, a way to keep their brain going and have a voice, or as an outlet to vent their experiences and frustrations with certain elements of motherhood.

We asked Kiran Chug from the Mumsnet Bloggers Network to tell us more about the Mummy blogging phenomenon and the network itself.

Ask the expert

Kiran Chug is the editor of the Mumsnet Bloggers Network.

How does Mumsnet Bloggers Network work?
We choose a mix of blog posts to highlight and share each day. There's the prestigious 'blog of the day', and then three other 'front page' posts which the Bloggers Network team pick out each morning. We

→

look for compelling writing across a range of subjects.

Once we've chosen the posts, we share a teaser or short excerpt for them on Mumsnet, and link out to the blogger's original post. Getting these daily slots can be great for bloggers – it can result in thousands of extra page views in a day and a new regular audience for bloggers.

How has the way in which mums get information contributed to the rise of Mummy blogging?

These days, mothers no longer buy a magazine to find out which is the best brand for a given product: now you can consult as many blogs as you've got time to read. What we are seeing is that readers are more likely to trust someone whose life echoes their own, and consumers are warier of messaging put together by a team of PR and advertising executives. In the blogosphere, you can read about a mother with children the same age as yours and hear her experience of road testing a product, rather than reading a lone journalist's account of trying a bunch of things and telling you her favourites.

Brands know women listen to other women, which means Mummy bloggers ARE taken seriously and can run viable businesses being bloggers, which in turn attracts more women to do the same thing.

'Follow your passions!'

I hear this so much, and while it's a good philosophy and I've talked about the importance of passion above, it does come with a word of caution!

For years we've seen an emerging call to 'live your life on your own terms' – turning your back on the corporate world of predictable careers and nine to five jobs and just following your dreams. And when you're researching your blog niche, it's very tempting to base your choice on this. After all, who wouldn't want to 'choose a job you love – and never have to "work" a day in your whole life'?

It is definitely true that blogging about your passion can be the one thing that keeps you going. Successful blogging takes huge amounts of dedication, hard work, drive and also determination to look to the horizon and keep going even when you feel like no one is actually reading your blog. It follows that it's much easier to persevere with a subject you are genuinely passionate about and would be talking about anyway.

However, before you commit the mortgage and your children's wellbeing to your new blog about growing magnolias in ceramic pots, remember this: if you realise that you've launched off in a direction that has no commercial opportunity or even audience, you quickly lose motivation or can't put in the necessary time. You most likely have real financial needs that can't be paid by passion alone, whether that is mortgages, rent, school fees, holidays . . .

The bloggers I have spoken to will all tell you that their success has not happened overnight, and in fact for some it has taken many years to get to the incredible situation they are in today. So you can see how it will benefit you to know that you have chosen a niche that combines your passions or interests with a viable audience and real monetisation pull.

So – look for the opportunity *within* your passions

The best advice is to strike a balance between passions and dreams and your own circumstances and everyday needs, and also focus on where opportunity lies within the world and crucially, where it can quickly be monetised.

Now, the good news is that whatever your passion, there *is* money, profit and wealth to be discovered and created from it; that is not in question. Even if you think of the most bizarre thing imaginable, there are people out there selling related services, products and information around it.

But your own circumstances might mean one of the following:

- You may need to start your blog around your existing job (which many of our bloggers in this book did). That working life devoted exclusively to your passion may have to wait in the short term.
- You may need to start blogging and learning about blogging around your existing area of expertise, thus driving consultancy work. This ties you into your current work for longer, but it also gives you invaluable experience.
- You may need to look across *all* your passions (most people have more than one!) and take a calculated and well thought out decision based on which passion is most likely to be able to be monetised the fastest.

You know what? All of these are still great ways forward. Bear in mind, even if you end up building a blog that is 95 per cent rather than 100 per cent your passion, there are still going to be all sorts of benefits to be had in terms of being your own boss, developing your own media brand and becoming well known. The opportunities and positioning that come from that can still be life changing and enhancing in many different ways.

Remember this fact too: passions don't stay the same throughout a lifetime. If I think back to the various things I have been passionate about in the past, it feels like they must have been the passions of a different person (the American boy band New Kids on the Block being a very good case in point).

Passions and interests are often driven by life stages and, as life moves on, so do your passions and interests. So don't get too caught up in the 'it's only about my passions' hype above all other considerations. This book is about the *business* of blogging and successful people always make calculated and well thought out decisions that combine where the opportunities lie with what they know about and which path will most likely lead to success.

It's still work . . .

It has been really interesting to hear so many of the successful bloggers in this book – even those who are blogging only about their passions – say the same thing: that although they are passionate about their blog and its topic, they still feel like they're working, and working very hard. Like any business, it requires effort, consistency and determination.

When a mission is your motivation . . .

We're talking about *successful* blogging and niches – and it would be wrong to focus entirely on money-making niches. I mentioned in Chapter 2 about blogging for personal authority and leadership. There's a branch of this that is driven by the desire to influence meaningful change.

A cause or mission can be just as powerful a motivator as cash – and can certainly have huge impact in terms of reaching an audience, spreading a message, and bringing understanding, support, compassion and help to a particular need.

So before we go any further, I'd like to share the story of 46-year-old Hayley Goleniowska and her blog *Downs Side Up*. Cornering and serving a niche is important for success, but in Hayley's instance her niche is not about money but about her mission.

Hayley Goleniowska started *Downs Side Up* (downssideup.com) in 2012 about her daughter Natalia (Natty), now nine, as a way of helping other parents with children who suffered from Down's Syndrome. But she's not only been able to change the life of her daughter – Natty was the first child with a disability to appear in a UK television advertising campaign for a clothing range – she's also won numerous awards, appeared in a recent BBC documentary, and has increased visibility and awareness for people with Down's Syndrome in both the parenting and wider community.

What's the motivation behind your blog?

Our motivation is our daughter Natalia. When she came into our lives we thought our lives were over, but we were completely wrong. One of the first things that crossed my mind when she was born was that she'd grow up to have really awful clothes and a horrible haircut – really old-fashioned stereotypes that just flashed into my head. It was my own fear and ignorance that got to us. We wasted a couple of years wrapping our heads around the words 'Down's Syndrome', and I often get emotional wishing I could go back and change those years. I blog to try to give other parents back those years by dispelling some of the myths and fears.

Does it make money?

I purposely chose not to make money out of my blog to keep the message pure. If I was a new mum looking for support, I wouldn't want it filled with adverts and sponsored posts. Offers flood in daily, but I don't think it's the right fit for me and my mission.

How quickly did it become a success?

It was very quick. I'd been writing various tips and advice for a while, but it was a post called 'What to Say when a Baby's Born with Down's Syndrome' that went viral. I realised that people really wanted to read about our emotional journey. Now the blog is just the hub in the middle of a much bigger movement that I'm at the heart of. I've written a book, done guest articles for medical journals, and created a series of resources for medical professionals and new parents. As soon as there's a story in the news about Downs testing, TV shows and the press will come to me. It's become a full-time job, even though it's all unpaid.

Tell us about Natty's modelling career.

I remember looking at the media and thinking, 'where are the children like Natty?' Children like her aren't seen. So I started writing around to local companies, saying how important inclusion is and how we all need to see ourselves represented in the media. I explained that

→

beauty comes in many forms and that our kids love funky clothes the same as the rest of the gang. I then sent a pic of Natty to see if they wanted her in their campaigns. I got lots of 'Oh, she's gorgeous but not what we are looking for' and then a few yes answers: Frugi, Scott Dunn Travel and JoJo Maman Bebe, then it all took off. Natty was spotted by Sainsbury, who cast her in their back-to-school uniform campaign which made all the national papers and was debated endlessly on television. In terms of the representation of disabled people in the media, we still have a way to go, but we're getting there. It would be nice to see wheelchair users in mainstream advertising.

What does she think of it all?

Natty thinks that all kids grow up with TV and modelling! She's had a massive confidence boost from it all. The blog has brought us an invitation to the Queen's Garden Party at Buckingham Palace, a champagne reception hosted by Mrs Cameron at No. 10 and Natty attended a fancy dress party at the Lord Mayor of London's house. We've also met more celebrities than I can remember, but Natty treats them all the same!

This is such an inspirational story, and a good reminder that whether for profit or change, a blog must have some genuine authenticity in it – you. So once you've decided who you are and what you have to offer, you need to design the next ingredient that most successful bloggers have got nailed – your personal brand.

Chapter 4

Discover your personal brand

It's a busy and noisy world . . .

. . . and you're about to become just one blogger in a sea of *millions*. Not just that – we all live in a culture defined by limited time and focus, in which we are constantly distracted by endless messages coming from all our social media feeds, our emails and all our messaging apps.

How are *you* going to stand out? How will *you* compete for and earn attention?

If it wasn't for your personal brand, you probably wouldn't. Your brand is part of what sets you apart and gives you your own edge, your own story, your own message and your own distinctiveness. To some degree, we're talking about niching right down on who *you* are, rather than your topic and audience, as we've already talked about.

Brands influence almost every part of our lives – leisure, health, lifestyle, business, investments – and create loyalty, emotional buy-in and especially the desire for more of the same. In the world of personal branding, the same thing can be achieved. The bloggers with great personal brands – think Zoella – have fans waiting for their video uploads and buying every product they endorse.

It's what makes you memorable, striking and defined. It's all the little things about you that give others the feeling that you are one-of-a-kind. It's what makes your audience connect with you and become loyal to you.

So, *combined with your niche*, your personal brand is what will really set your blog (or business blog) apart and that is why having a clear idea of both is so important. Your personal brand is what will make you be seen as highly visible, credible and valuable and what will bring you more money, opportunity, fun and success.

What is branding?

In the world of business, a brand is anything that you identify to distinguish one product from another – a symbol, a colour scheme, reputation, employees, etc. Marketing uses it to differentiate a product and give it a perceived competitive edge. But a business brand also tells a story and includes the good – the experience your customers have and your amazing products – and the bad – the PR disasters a company suffers. Brand is inseparably linked to loyalty, and brand is something that has to be managed as well as created.

And what is personal branding?

We already each have a personal brand even if we don't always realise it. Think of the way you choose to dress and the interests you choose to share on social media. But your personal brand creeps into the tougher parts of life too. Just as with business, we need to be mindful of our own branding when we're interviewing for a job, climbing up the corporate ladder or looking for freelance work online – and it's especially true when you are a blogger and looking to stand out online.

Branding is very powerful. Just as we can learn to like, trust and understand big brands such as Apple and Nike, so we can develop similar emotions, feelings and understanding about *people*. Those with great personal brands are influencers, almost casting a spell over their devoted audience. We buy their products, listen to their wisdom and follow their advice.

So, as a blogger, your personal branding is essentially what you are known for and what people seek you out for, as illustrated in Shaa's story.

Shaa Wasmund MBE (follow her blog at shaa.com) is an entrepreneur and author of two best-selling books, *Stop Talking Start Doing* and *Do Less, Get More*. In 2015, she built a personal brand through blogging, social media and education in the entrepreneurship niche. Her results have been phenomenally successful: selling 10,000 online courses generating over $1m in recurring revenue; training over 1000 people in business through workshops and award-winning retreats. She was recently named one of the UK's Top 20 Most Influential Entrepreneurs by *The Sunday Times*, is a regular guest reading the papers on Sky News, has a column in *Psychologies Magazine* and flew out to Necker Island by personal invitation of Sir Richard Branson.

→

What is a personal brand and why is it so important?

Your personal brand is everything. It's your #1 asset. Most businesses can be copied and there's almost certainly somebody that offers the same factual services as you – so your true differentiator is *you*. We all buy from the brands that we're attracted to, that speak our language, that show they care about what we care about and make us feel special. The authentic personal brands that are the real deal and speak to us don't need to sell to us: we queue up to buy from them.

How important is your blog to your personal brand?

The look of your website and the content on it is your window to the world, so I can't tell you how important it is. Every day I meet people with awful websites who're telling me they need more customers, that they're not converting visitors to buyers and are spending too much on marketing . . . the answer is always that their website isn't working hard enough for them to do any of this.

I wasted a lot of time redoing my website and once had three different versions in the space of six months. It was worth it in the end though. But if I was just starting out and had any money to invest I'd spend it getting my website ready right from the off. Otherwise you set the wrong impression and end up spending more time and money redoing it.

Your website needs to showcase what you do and what you stand for, and needs to provide a powerful 'ethical bribe' to convince visitors to opt in so you can grow a list and provide them with value in order to nurture those subscribers into repeat buyers. More than anything you need to be really proud of it! Don't settle for something you know isn't up to scratch and you are ashamed of – it'll undermine all the good you do elsewhere.

What one action has had the biggest impact in the growth of your personal brand, and why?

It was writing my first book. But I didn't set out to write any old book – I set out to write a #1 best-seller. I was very, very clear about that. I invested heavily and spent over $10,000 on Tim Ferriss's authors' retreat and discovered exactly how the world's best-selling authors market their books and build huge digital audiences around what they do. Let's face it, you don't make money from the books, it's the opportunities that the books present you. No way would I have got the press and media opportunities I've had without my books. Books are a fantastic way to grow your personal brand, position yourself as an expert, reach a bigger audience, spread your message further and charge a premium for your services.

Where should people start?

Start by asking yourself a few questions:

- What do you stand for ... what are your values?
- What are the things that really annoy or frustrate you? Note: You will often find these are in direct conflict with your most important values!
- What are your passions? Talk about them and share them.

→

- How can you truly serve your customers?
- What exact line of work do you want to be known for? Think 'the best gluten-free baker' rather than 'baker', or 'the new mums' fitness coach' rather than 'fitness coach'.
- How can I take the skills, knowledge and expertise I've already got and make money online?
- How can I produce online courses or products to build a scalable business helping 1000s of people rather than constantly working 1:1 and trading all my time for money?

How much effort do you put into content creation?

Content is our #1 priority in the business and tactic for social media. All our marketing is content. Content is how we reach people, bring them to our site, engage with them and convince them to give us their email address. It's how we showcase the value we can deliver and is how we nurture and build trust until people want to work with us. Content tells our story and is the difference between us *telling* people what we do and *showing* people what we do. You simply can't choose not to create content anymore – and that's a good thing.

So what makes up your personal brand?

Again, let's take our cue from normal life. When you first meet someone and begin to get to know them you absorb all kinds of information about them and this creates your initial impressions.

You're sizing up their 'personal brand' – studies show the conclusions you reach in the first five minutes will play a role in determining your relationship over the long term.

It's just the same with your online brand – but online there are multiple touch points at which someone might begin to form that impression ... your website, your social media profiles, your email signature, your tweets, your Facebook updates, and that's just the start.

Your personal brand *also* includes your values, your reputation and your talents – it's how you behave, how you talk and what makes you compelling. It's what you're known for and how people experience you. It includes your story, how you appear to the world. It is what makes you, you – and it's how your audience, clients and customers feel about you.

So who are you – really?

Understanding the 'personal brand' concept is one thing, pinning down your own is quite another! This isn't surprising when you think how many of us have stumbled into careers and then woken up 10 years down the line thinking *'Why am I actually an accountant/hairdresser/sales manager...?'*

However, powerful personal brands don't happen by accident. Now you're preparing for your blogging career, you need to make some very careful and deliberate decisions. Defining your brand means defining a vision of yourself – and then taking the steps towards bringing that vision to life. Fortunately, there is a method for doing this and it involves creating your all-important brand mission statement.

Your personal brand mission statement

Ideally, once you've finished the rest of this chapter, you should be able to complete the following sentence:

I am a

_____

(lawyer, hairdresser, dog walker, etc. – how you see yourself professionally or your blogging niche, i.e. beauty blogger, lifestyle blogger)

who _____

_____

(describe your unique talents and viewpoints and how you use them)

for _____

_____

(describe who your target audience are)

so they can _____

_____

_____

(describe the desired experience or results you want to give to your audience)

You'll end up with one or two sentences defining you, what you're good at, who you're serving and the unique experience you are giving your audience.

You don't necessarily need to publish this anywhere – it's just for your own reference, a personal brand statement that is distinctive to you and you alone. If you think of the strapline or catchphrase that famous household products have, then this is your own personal equivalent.

You can even use it to create a tagline that you decide to use, as Evan Carmichael has done.

Evan Carmichael blogs in the entrepreneurship niche with the goal of helping a billion entrepreneurs to start or build businesses. He is considered one of the leading global social media talents by Forbes – his website (evancarmichael.com) contains over 70,000 pages of content by 8000 authors and attracts 400,000 visitors per month, and he has published 3000 videos on YouTube.

Evan, tell us about your tagline 'Believe'.

My tagline for ages was 'motivation and strategies for entrepreneurs'. It tells you what I do – but it was so boring! It's what everybody says and it doesn't have an emotional connection. I didn't like my tagline but I didn't know why, and for a long time I couldn't figure out how to fix it. I started writing down a list of taglines, and 'Believe' was one of them – but, or so I thought, it was too short. However, I kept coming back to it. In the end I realised that 'Believe' is my personality, the one word that represents my brand and it goes into everything I do. It's at the heart of the content I create, of what I inspire others to do. It's in my logo design – I have an aeroplane flying upwards to signify growth, and at the end of my videos I do an upwards hand gesture which is all about belief and growing. Everything that

→

I create is about 'Believe' and I apply belief to the entrepreneurship niche.

Does everyone need a tagline?

A tagline is a positioning statement and helps other people understand what you're about and helps them talk about you in an easy way. Lots of things help – using Twitter, and having a YouTube channel – and having a tagline helps too.

Evan, you've created so much content – how do you keep going?

I enjoyed the process. I've made 3000 videos now, but it wasn't easy. For the first 700 or so, I embarrassed myself. I was so bad I couldn't watch them back. Each day I focused on being better than I was the day before. It took me 1300 videos until I motivated myself – I watched a video and was like 'wow, that's good' – but it took me that long! People give up too early. I see people who are just five videos into their own series and already thinking, 'I'm so bad' – so I say, 'if I showed you *my* fifth video, you'd see you're way better than I was!' – so go with the process, and focus on getting better every day and enjoying the journey.

Your personal brand pillars

Don't expect to build a personal brand overnight or have one handed to you on a plate. It will take time and it's a step-by-step, piece-by-piece process, both online and offline within the industry and niche in which you operate. But the results will be well worth the effort.

To make it easier, I want you to think in terms of *personal brand pillars*, described below. Some of these may appear to overlap directly with your niche – that's fine. But there is a difference – whilst your niche is about your subject matter, your personal brand is about *you*, it's where 'you' the blog owner sit alongside the 'what' of the blog topic.

Pillar 1: Your strengths, values and mission
Pillar 2: Your image
Pillar 3: Your authenticity and trust factor
Pillar 4: Your opinions

Pillar 1: Your strengths, values and mission

People with strong brands are clear about who they are, their strengths, what they value and what their mission is. They know what they know about, who they can help and how they can help.

But it's no use if only *you* know your strengths and your mission; other people need to know them too. So clarify them on your 'about' page on your blog, communicate them in your posts and across social media and online profiles, and seek opportunities that allow you to showcase and demonstrate your strengths.

If you're unsure what your strengths are, ask those around you what they think of you. There are various online tools such as Survey Monkey that you can use to allow your friends and family to answer your questions anonymously. What do they say are your strengths?

Pillar 2: Your image

This isn't about being a supermodel, but it *is* about looking the part and walking the talk. Of all the things that make up a personal brand, image is one of the most important – it's about putting your shirt and tie on.

First impressions happen in the blink of an eye (studies show people reach conclusions about other people in less than a second based on things such as attractiveness, likeability and capability) – this occurs with first impressions of you, as you go out and about in the real world and the impression you make online.

Audiences are increasingly visual, preferring to look at pictures rather than read words – you only have to look at the runaway success of Instagram and Pinterest to realise just how much. That's why I always insist on a great-looking blog and great-looking photography for anyone who wants to build a strong personal brand, be known as a talented influencer or the best in their industry, and be seen as someone you can really trust and who deserves handsome fees for speaking at events. As a blogger, the first place most people are going to meet you is online, so you've got to start with photography and branding elements such as your logo and colour scheme, which need to be consistent across all your online platforms.

The good news is that whilst you might have a hundred things to say about yourself in words, pictures can get the message across just as well. Of course you can use words to say 'I'm successful, I'm confident, I'm a leader, I'm stylish, I'm a foodie, I'm friendly, I'm approachable' – and every text-based post you make will reinforce this – but if you have a great photographer you can say all of that in a single image *and* get the message across instantly.

Don't forget action shots! Great photography for your blog doesn't have to stop with a profile shot. Whatever you're doing online, put more of yourself into it and let's see you in action! Action shots are great, whether it's you talking at an event in your niche, sitting on the front row next to Anna Wintour or showing up outside Downing Street to talk to the PM.

It doesn't have to be glamorous or have a 'wow factor' – you just need action shots that provide instant visual proof and confirmation of your expertise and knowledge. So, if you meet someone you admire, get a photo alongside them and write a blog post about it. Or if you're at an event that serves your niche, get a photo of you standing by the entrance. It's all about showing you are living and breathing whatever it is you are blogging about. You're showing up. You're connected. You're a genuine part of that world. Behind the scenes imagery giving glimpses into your world works well too.

Chris's story focuses on the importance of being yourself – and inevitably that includes some powerful advice about using photography to reinforce a credible personal brand.

Chris Brogan is a *New York Times* best-selling author of nine books, and marketing consultant and owner of Owner Media. His clients include PepsiCo, Disney, General Motors, Microsoft and more. Through his blog at chrisbrogan.com, opinions and imagery, he has built a powerful personal brand that drives business and digital marketing consulting opportunities and has made him a global influencer in the digital marketing niche.

→

Tell us about your personal brand and how it drives opportunity.

My personal brand is built on a really simple premise: be helpful. So I share as much as I can of the 'good stuff' that most other people charge you to see or hear. This has led to many people deciding I should be part of their storyline in some way and wanting to work with me. I also use images of myself in most of my blog posts, and I use a mix of professional photography alongside selfie images. I think being controlled about your image is so twenty years ago – be yourself, why try to pretend you're something you're not?

What role does your blog play in your personal brand?

In the beginning, I just saw my blog as magic. I could connect with people and share ideas and it was this great tool that let me reach out and be part of many conversations and storylines. Today, I see my blog as being integral to my personal brand. I got my first book deal in 2009 based on the success of the blog. I still don't look at my site itself as a money-maker directly – I use it as a calling card for whatever else I'm doing, it's a communications tool. I make money via speeches, via consulting and via advisory roles that quite often start with someone discovering my blog and my personal brand.

Having a personal brand and putting yourself out there can be frightening. What is your advice?

Fear is a very powerful motivator. It drives pretty much everything. Fear isn't the enemy. It's a great tool. If you learn how to embrace fear, you gain an ally. Be afraid. Then do it anyway.

I sound dumb often. People disagree with me often. I'm wrong often. Guess what happens? Not a lot. I just keep doing what I do. I can tell you that the most successful people I know are all willing to admit they don't know much. The least successful people I know are the ones who tell me how smart they are. I just strive to be helpful – and success is the by-product.

Pillar 3: Your authenticity and trust factor

Authenticity is a huge buzzword in the blogosphere. Official definitions of authenticity include: 'Real or genuine; not copied or false; true and accurate; made to be or look like an original.' In the business world whole brands can be destroyed overnight if they're shown to have lied or mis-sold what they offer. But it matters just as much in personal branding too.

Both individually and collectively we are all really good at spotting when something is fake. We get a funny feeling about a person, we know something is off and we start taking what someone says with a pinch of salt. The easiest way to avoid this is simply to be authentic, to genuinely be, behave and act like yourself rather than trying to be something you're not.

Now, there is one way in which personal and business brands differ – your personal brand is allowed to show imperfections. In fact, it can often be one of the enduringly appealing parts of your brand because it's so obviously real. What you might see as your own imperfections might even mark the start of a booming business. Stephanie and Adrienne Vendetti are sisters, natural-born redheads and co-founders of the blog *How To Be A Redhead* (howtobearedhead.com). Their blog empowers every red-haired woman to feel confident and look amazing. Both sisters had been bullied over the colour of their hair, with one even going blonde to 'fit in'. Now they are at the helm of a beauty empire and community that provides top beauty and fashion advice for redheads around the globe, have been L'Oréal brand ambassadors, have their own book, are embarking on a tour of the US and have been featured in media outlets from the *New York Times* to the *Daily Mail*. Their story illustrates that you can embrace your quirks and the little things that make you different. It's all about being *you*.

Pillar 4: Your opinions

Opinions are just that, opinions, not fact. But, well-presented and articulated within a balanced argument, they are worthy of sharing – your opinions will define and power your brand *and* keep your blog alive.

I'd like to tell you a story about Dr Zoe Norris, a GP in East Yorkshire. You might know of Dr Norris from the Channel 4 series 'NHS £2 Billion A Week and Counting' and also her appearances on *Newsnight*, *BBC Breakfast*, Radio 5 Live and local radio. She speaks as a voice for the staff and patients who work for and use the NHS daily and know the reality of the current health service.

The question is, why Zoe? Why, out of the hundreds of thousands of GPs in the UK, has she ended up building a personal brand that has led to her becoming a spokesperson for her industry and the NHS?

The answer is her opinion, and in particular sharing her opinion on a platform that reaches millions of people. Zoe

Norris is a regular blogger on the *Huffington Post*, where her articles include 'The NHS wars, who is to blame' and 'Why I don't want a seven day NHS treating my family'.

She started blogging because she felt passionately about what was happening to the NHS – and everything she writes is personal and thought provoking but also strikes a chord with patients and doctors alike. Through writing regularly, passionately and in a language everyone can understand, and on a huge global platform, she has not only raised public awareness of the issues she knows about but has been picked out by TV producers who want her opinions – thus she has become a spokesperson and leader in her industry.

Using your opinion to build your profile and personal brand is also known as thought leadership.

So, if you have an opinion and you can get it out there in a sustained and consistent way, then cross-posting the content you create for your own blog onto a platform like the Huffington Post can make a huge difference to your reach, authority and the way others perceive you.

Most niches have large news-style websites (such as Forbes, Entrepreneur and Lifehack) that allow other people to contribute – and your opinions and willingness to share them and lead your industry help make you distinctive. Also, as we'll see in Chapter 9, getting your posts published on larger sites that aggregate content from different sources (known as guest-blogging) is a useful route to getting more traffic to your own site.

Ask the expert

Jody Thompson is the UK Blogs Editor for the *Huffington Post*. She oversees the UK community of bloggers on the *Huffington Post,* which includes people from all walks of life who want to get their voice heard – politicians, students, professionals, professors, entertainers, activists, heads of non-profit organisations, etc.

How can a blogger catch your attention?
I get around 500 emails a day. To catch my eye, you need to stand out immediately from the subject box of your email. A good header for your email would say 'Blog pitch' and then I know 'it's about a blog pitch'. If you can follow that with a five-word summary of your pitch, even better. So for instance: Blog Pitch: Why Climate Change must go on the Agenda. Inside the email, I am not interested in hearing your life story. Generally, I'm looking for a brief summary of the blog post or even better the blog post itself.

Are there any topics that you think are overdone?
I think all subjects go round and round, but there is always room for fresh voices that will make a blog post go crackers. For example, you could argue that parenting has been done to death as a blog topic, but those posts really fly. One topic that did very well recently was breastfeeding – another topic you'd think had run out of steam – but a number of our bloggers were responding to Jamie Oliver's comments on breastfeeding, and being topical the posts went viral.

How do you advise people to come up with ideas?

A good place to look for inspiration is what is going on in the news. We are always open to new voices sharing their opinion on what is going on in the day for any of our verticals, which include politics, comedy, style, tech, entertainment and young voices. The key to any blog is to showcase passion.

And for professional people?

If you are the head of a business, write a post about something that relates to your expertise without directly promoting your business, such as 'Why Entrepreneurs Should Throw Away Business Manuals'. Your goal is to think of the human angle to your specific expertise. If you run a sleep centre, you could write '10 tips to get more sleep'. Put your content over promotion. All bloggers get a link and bio at the end of the article so you are raising awareness of what you do without obviously promoting yourself.

What makes posts go viral?

Now that is the million dollar question! That said, you can read certain blogs and you know they will fly. I would say it comes down to passion, newsworthiness such as hitting a particular trend or topic that people are keen to read about that day, and it's about whether the post starts a conversation.

What is important for bloggers to remember when pitching to you?

We don't change or edit the titles to your posts, so think carefully about the title. Is it compelling? Why would anyone read this? And don't give up. Every single blog

→

pitch is taken on its individual merit. Every blogger has their day. Some bloggers will pitch posts that are not so good, and then they come along with a really great post that goes straight up on the front page.

Using opinions for authority

What do you do if you can't quite believe that you're allowed to have your own opinions?

It's a dilemma I see often – people who find it scary to admit to and share their opinions or point of view, as if they have no validity. Someone recently asked me 'Am I allowed to have an opinion on what is happening in my industry?' The answer is YES, YES, YES!

I think this insecurity comes from the way that blogging has completely reversed the way we have always expected things to happen.

Traditionally, whether in our working corporate lives, at school or even simply at home as young children, we were always asked for our opinions – we were not encouraged to offer them unsolicited. It's just like the way that we were selected for promotions and opportunities rather than being expected to go out seeking them. Generally, throughout our lives and particularly for those of us who grew up in the world before the digital landscape of today, you kept schtum until someone else anointed you with the privilege of whatever it was you were looking for: they asked if you'd speak at an event, they'd invite you to write for their publication, they'd select you for promotion.

But the internet and blogging has turned all of that on its head. What we see with blog stars and leaders now is that *they* take the decision to stand up and be counted, to have an opinion, to put it out there and to keep putting it out there – and their raised and enhanced personal brand and profile follows from that initial confidence and mind set. They don't wait for someone else to ask them or to be granted permission. They just take a decision and use their own voice – we're not necessarily talking about controversial opinions, just opinions. You can be a beauty blogger and you have an opinion on a product. Your opinion is yours alone and in having that opinion, you are demonstrating that you are a leader.

So – if you're hesitating about the worth of your own opinions, here are five easy tricks to help you grow more comfortable with it, to grow from where you are today to a thought leader in your niche. Of course, it is all to do with content creation.

1. Use the news cycle of your industry, and turn it on its head

Whatever industry you are in, there is always industry news – so keep on top of all your industry publications and what they are talking about as there will always be hidden opportunities to find an original, personal angle that stands out.

One of my clients, a fashion consultant for example, wants to be a fresh voice in a luxury fashion industry that is currently full of doom and gloom. The news is all about how it's over for luxury fashion, with several high profile fashion label closures. Now, if my client joins the fray talking about how it's all belt-tightening from here for luxury fashion, her voice will get lost in the noise. So instead, she can turn the story on its head with ideas such as 'Why there has never been a better time than 2016 to launch a luxury fashion line' (and obviously backing this up with a load of credible and relevant reasons). After all, the closure of one or two large labels isn't going to stop hundreds of people opening new labels – so why not try to be a positive and uplifting voice amongst the negativity?

2. Move an industry story on to its next chapter

A different way of launching on the back of what's hot and current in your news sector is to develop the story further rather than challenging it. Stories don't really end – every story is linear and there is always something else that can happen next. In the case of the closure of high profile fashion brands, I'm no fashion expert but I doubt it marks the end of the entire industry – nor the story! Opinion blog posts could take up the next chapter in a number of ways: new up and coming labels have more space to come to market, fashion industry reaction, what's next for the designer? etc.

3. Offer an analysis of a topical situation

Another story in the fashion industry, seemingly all the time, is the fortunes of M&S. Whether you're a fashion blog star or a fashion consultant blogging to raise your profile with the brands who might hire you, you will have lots of say on this topic from what M&S do right, what they do wrong, what you would advise them to do. Your thoughts and views on a topical situation demonstrate that you are a leader in this field.

4. Offer a solution to an industry problem

Part of being a thought leader is to be the person who always seems to have the answer to a problem. You'll see this all the time in the national papers. But do these commentators who are called on to proffer solutions to problems really know best? Probably not. They just have the nerve to act like they do and can talk about it in an interesting and engaging way, promoting further discussion.

So what problems are there in your industry and what solutions can you offer? It doesn't have to be the best solution in the world, just something that provides food for thought and is well argued. Solutions are often subjective and there might be hundreds of different solutions to any given problem. No one is going to hold a gun to your head if your hypothetical solution isn't right! Probably no one will act on it at all, but the net result is that simply offering up a solution helps to position you as an industry leader.

5. Consistency

If only thought leadership were as simple as publishing a single killer blog post and suddenly becoming 'industry famous' with a load of opportunities falling at your feet. Well, it's not! Building personal brands takes time and so you have to keep creating content and publishing it over and over again. The four ideas above all require one quality if you're to use them effectively – consistency.

If you consistently offer sane, sensible, grounded commentary, you'll get known for it. The key is consistency – and it will raise your profile and strengthen your personal brand.

Even better, your consistency will resonate both within your niche and beyond. So while you'll gain authority and respect as a leader, you'll also be sought out by the media as a commentator.

Journalists are always looking for well-regarded people with opinions who can give arguments and counter arguments and who can move existing stories on. By creating content along the lines of the above, you are stamping out and establishing your personal brand piece by piece and proving you're able to do what journalists need you to do.

This has been a necessarily long and detailed chapter. So I'd like to end with some succinct advice from Nick Gold.

Ask the expert

Nick Gold is the MD of Speaker's Corner and the European Association of Speaker Bureaus (EASB). His clients are corporations willing to spend up to £100k on the right speaker and Nick knows what makes a great personal brand.

Here are his top tips for creating yours.

Don't reinvent the wheel
Bloggers often think they need shock value and a really strong opinion to differentiate themselves. But those with the strongest personal brands don't necessarily have different opinions – it is more about clear opinions and thought-processes. Don't worry if the message isn't unique, clarity is more important.

Try to speak on behalf of your audience
You don't have to put out new and crazy ideas. You have to put out ideas that make your audience think: 'That is exactly what I think and I wish I could articulate it like that.'

Strong personal brands include warts and all

Think of your experience watching Olympic 100m finalists. If you just watch the race, the emotion and connection you feel is limited. If you hear that person tell you how they had to drag themselves out of bed on a cold winter morning having not seen their kids for a month, but they did it because of what they wanted to achieve, your connection is more powerful. Success stories used to be just about your success, now they are about your real story. Your audience wants to see your whole journey. You don't have to hide behind the facade of success – people like other people to be real and transparent.

You don't have to know all the answers

We live in a world where people crave information and we have a huge surplus of information and opinion. Even if you are a huge expert at what you do, don't pretend to know it all. By being an expert, what you are doing is saying: 'I'm giving you the information that I understand and I have credibility and you can choose what to conclude and how to use it.'.

Chapter 5

Show me the money

If you're reading this book, you are thinking about blogging as a business. While many blogs still begin as passion projects, outlets for creativity or frustration, we've already seen that there are plenty of people who find that after a few years they have a lucrative business on their hands.

So, let's put our business heads on. The lifeblood of any business is the act of selling to generate incoming money. As the business owner you can chase these sales in many different ingenious ways and using any number of different products and offers (as long as they are legal of course!). But your customers need to find you ...

Let's talk traffic

In stark terms, your blog is simply a means to attract online traffic – potential customers who you or your paying advertisers want to reach and sell to – and that traffic only comes to your blog if those people are interested in what you write about. Hence even the most fabulous-looking blog, packed with life-enhancing messages and prize-winning content, will have no commercial value unless it attracts traffic. Without traffic you just have a blog, with traffic you also have a blog with earning potential that can become a business. We'll be talking a lot more about traffic in Chapter 8 but for now, bear in mind that more traffic equals more opportunity in all the different monetisation routes, and that how much traffic you need depends on how much income you are trying to get.

Look around you and learn . . .

I live in London's Notting Hill and when it comes to seeing business and opportunity in action, I love walking through its famous Portobello Road Market. In fact, I always find myself thinking how if the government really wants to encourage entrepreneurship in the UK, they should get all school children to spend a month in a place like Portobello Road Market – testing ideas, selling and talking to people, but that's another story.

So, in Portobello Market, you have plenty of 'traffic', including the tourists that cram the streets on Fridays and Saturdays. The local council could definitely do more to get more traffic to the area, just as you as a blog owner will be able to do things to improve the traffic to your blog.

Nonetheless, because there are lots of visitors to the area, all sorts of business owners step up to predict and serve the needs of these tourists, try to engage them and get money off them. From the stallholders selling every product under the sun to the café owners providing refreshments, from the advertisers who pay premiums to have their ads at Notting Hill Gate station to the street performers and mime artists who put on informal shows and collect money in hats – they're all making money from traffic.

With the sheer number and variety of visitors to Portobello Market, the only limit to how those entrepreneurs derive an income is their imagination. It's the same with your blog – your blog traffic is just like these tourists who walk down Portobello Road – and, like all those businesses, remember there is no one rule or method when it comes to monetisation.

Sounds simple – but in reality . . .

Most people don't fully understand the complexities of blog monetisation. Most potential bloggers, if asked, would cite banner adverts placed by brands as the chief source of income. But they are just one small part of a much bigger picture and in fact are looking increasingly vulnerable as adblocking (more on this later) technology comes into force.

The most sophisticated bloggers today continually look for new routes to monetisation and never stop thinking about creative ways to drive an income and earnings from their work.

So, you need to learn about the main forms of blogging income – and also learn from the stories in this book about how important it is to keep looking for new ways. One thing we all know about the internet and online communication is that it is constantly evolving – and so must anyone who wants to earn money from it. The good news is that you have extraordinary freedom and flexibility – as you will discover, many of the bloggers we meet in this book combine some or all the methods below to create a recession-proof business with diverse streams of income.

How to earn money from your blog

What follows is loosely organised in the order in which different stages of income *tend* to happen for bloggers, but nothing is set in stone with blogging.

How quickly you start to earn money depends on your own goals and the approach you want to take. Some bloggers won't even consider running ads for brands until they have built a large audience that loves their blogs; others run ads from the beginning, taking the view that it's easier to integrate the commercial apparatus from the start and learn about ads as they go along, and that they might as well make it apparent from the off that the blog is a commercial one (and who knows, they may make some money right from the start). On the other hand, some bloggers don't just run third-party ads from the start, they also promote their *own* products that they sell from the site.

It's confusing, isn't it? For now, just take comfort from knowing that while the blog is a business, its sources of revenue need not be set in stone at this point or at any point. So if you start by blogging about face cream but then find your blog evolves and opens up an opportunity to earn money by connecting banana sellers in Timbuktu with shopkeepers in Tasmania, then go for it.

Income from blogs falls into two distinct spheres – *direct* earnings and *indirect* earnings. Direct earnings come from advertising, selling your own products or helping to sell other companies' products and I'll explain later in the chapter how you can set this up; indirect earnings come from tangible opportunities that arise as a result of your blog's success.

However, rather than introducing first one group and then the other, I'm not going to deal with one group and then the other. Instead I'll introduce these monetising opportunities in the order they might typically present themselves to you as you start to develop your blog. But remember, commercial blogging is extremely versatile so don't be surprised if your own commercial journey follows a different route.

Affiliate marketing (direct earnings)

Affiliate marketing is the process of earning a commission by promoting or recommending other people's or companies' products. Essentially, you find a product you like, promote it to your audience and when a sale is made, you'll earn a piece of the profit.

Now this is something you could do from the outset as, even if you have just gained your first reader, who's to say that reader won't buy something you recommend or talk about?

Affiliate advertising is big business – it's incredible how many brands, both online and real world, now offer affiliate programmes to pay commission to those who generate sales for them. Pretty much everyone. What works really well, however, is to focus on higher-priced products – or to keep a really sharp focus on your chosen niche (see Chapter 4). This way, even if you still have quite modest traffic, you can earn significant commissions on individual sales – perhaps as a chef talking about expensive kitchen products or a car blogger who is reviewing and recommending cars.

Of course you first need to establish a commercial relationship with the brand or company, either by getting in touch direct or by being referred by affiliate partners such as Skimlinks or Affiliate Window that represent thousands of different merchants who might like you as an affiliate. Percentages vary between brands, products and the deals that you strike.

A word of caution: Once you begin affiliate marketing it is very easy to get carried away – suddenly you see every high-priced product as a revenue opportunity even if it is not remotely related to the topic of your blog. Before you know it you have turned your blog into a messed-up incoherent catalogue and you lose traffic as people no longer find focus, value and reward in visiting it.

You must consider your audience and what they are looking for *and* you must feature products you fully believe in. Every blogger interviewed for this book has talked about the importance of authenticity and of the reader's uncanny ability to see through a blogger who's just in it for a fast buck and not committed to offering real entertainment value and information.

Consulting, services, bookings or coaching (indirect earnings)

By writing your blog you are in effect marketing yourself, telling the world that you have experience and knowledge. If that includes professional services that you can sell, there will be plenty of people ready to pay you if your blog convinces them of your superior expertise. For example, I blog about digital strategy for helping grow small businesses and personal profiles, and my blog convinces potential clients that I am the person to work with.

As a provider of professional services you will gain more visibility through blogging than those who don't. But there's another benefit too – with a good-looking blog and regular content you can be seen as a *premium* service provider and raise your prices accordingly.

Think of it like this: imagine I'm looking for something really simple – someone to help train my new puppy. As a modern connected consumer, I'm definitely going to research on the internet, but I first open a static website that doesn't tell me much or let me interact with it. Then I hit upon a blog site that showcases all their training techniques with plenty of great photos and videos of them with happy-looking dogs and a run of their success stories. No prizes for guessing which one I'll take notice of. We'll be talking a lot more about blogging for business in Chapter 11.

Freelance blogging (indirect earnings)

Many of the bloggers I've talked to stumbled into an unexpected revenue source in their early days. Without them intending it to, their blog was advertising their writing talents – and suddenly they found themselves with paid writing jobs for other businesses. They continued to develop their own blog, building their personal profile and writing about their chosen niche or passion, but earned useful money ghost-blogging for someone who wanted a bit of the same digital marketing power.

All businesses (as we'll see in Chapter 11) need to be blogging and have their digital strategy completely nailed, but many don't have the time to blog or don't know what to write. It's a job they prefer to outsource and in their eyes the ideal person to write it is the person whose blog they absolutely love. Even if the subject matter is different, writing is writing.

So, you may not keep it up forever but writing for other people can be a good way to earn money from your blog while you're still getting it established.

Banner ads (direct earnings)

Once you reach a certain level of traffic, your blog becomes attractive to brands and companies as valuable advertising space. Blog owners normally charge advertisers a fixed fee for a certain time period, or base the fee on the number of times the advert actually appears (impressions).

You get the most money if you sell adverts direct to advertisers, but you can also use advertising networks who sell your ad space on your behalf and take commission. Google AdSense, for example, is a popular ad network through which Google places ads on your site. If you post videos in your blog you can also monetise those by allowing Google to run their adverts ahead of your videos.

Blog post sponsorship deals (direct earnings)

Brands are always looking for subtle but effective ways of getting in front of an audience and promoting their products. One way is to partner with a blogger who is then paid to write a piece reviewing or discussing their product (this is NOT the same as writing your *own* impartial reviews as part of your mainstream independent content). The job of the blogger is to take the brand's brief or product, and then create content around that product in their own persona and voice, in a way that their audience will accept and enjoy. All the bloggers we have talked to look for creative ways to cover the brand's topic in a way that works for their audience, feels natural, and doesn't sound like a hard sell.

Digital products (direct earnings)

Digital products are e-courses, e-books, paid-for audio or video products – and they form a huge market. Right now, digital courses delivered by video are hugely popular. So if you build up a great personal brand and establish your expertise, you can use it to sell digital products of your choice that you have created. Businesses can also sell digital products through their blogs, especially training products that complement their real world services.

Trust me, all around the world people are making incredible money selling digital courses on everything and anything you can imagine. You can even create a membership website into which you release new courses or information and charge people a subscription to join. To give an example, I know a watercolour artist who raises her profile by blogging about her latest projects and techniques, and who has hundreds of people paying to be a part of her membership website where she uploads video lessons and workbooks to teach people to paint as well as she does. Because of her membership club, she certainly does not fit the bill of poverty-stricken artist.

As the author of a digital product, you get all the money! Even better, make the product 'evergreen' – a popular word in the blogosphere which means the product won't date easily – and you can keep selling it for years and years.

If you think how much information is available for free on Google, it seems amazing that anyone would pay for information at all, but they do, in their millions. It doesn't even matter if other people are selling the same or similar products – once people connect to you through your blog, it's *your* take and opinion on how to do things that they want, not anyone else's.

You can design your course to be as long or as short as you like, you can auto-deliver it in weekly modules or let them download it all in one go, and you can include video demonstrations or audio commentaries too.

Branded products (direct earnings)

If you're feeling adventurous you can create branded products associated with your blog. Many of the bloggers in this book have product ranges from books to apps to craft kits and beauty lines. Popular examples include software, T-shirts and accessories. However, the key to doing this successfully is to make sure your product is closely related to your blog's topic so that it feels like a natural extension of your brand and something for your fans to be excited about rather than a cold sell just to earn money.

Apps (indirect earnings)

Once you're living and breathing the online and digital world, expect to spot new opportunities in the tech space. You might decide that your blog products or services could be delivered through a paid-for app, or spot a hole in the app market for one that you could create (I highly recommend reading George Berkowski's brilliant book *How to Build a Billion Dollar App* to find out more).

Speaking and book deals (indirect earnings)

As the new celebrities of our era, bloggers with huge numbers of social media followers find all kinds of opportunities that would previously have been reserved for film stars and sports heroes. These include book deals with real world publishers. In fact, this book you are reading right now came about, at least in part, because of the way my blog demonstrates my expertise in digital strategy.

For highly paid speaking opportunities, the world can be your oyster if you're a respected expert. Seth Godin is a case in point illustrating both of these income avenues – his blog isn't monetised but, as he said earlier in this book, it brings him incredible opportunities and has enabled him to write 18 successful books.

Writing for magazines and television presenting (indirect earnings)

As a former journalist, I can tell you that a lot of people in the traditional print industries are pretty peeved that bloggers are suddenly being offered articles to write and guest spots on popular daytime TV programmes. BUT WHO CARES? That, my friend, is just the way the cookie crumbles. You earn yourself a following and a status and if a magazine or TV show has noticed you and wants to pay you to contribute to their programme, then so be it!

Bonus! Free products . . .

OK, so not strictly cash in the bank, but once you're being offered free holidays, make-up, laptops, cars, computers, cinema tickets or whatever products fit with your blog, it certainly means you can live the good life *and* save a lot of income for other things!

Now, I'd like to introduce you to one of the most extraordinary bloggers in the western world, Grant Cardone, who uses his blog to drive numerous diverse income streams.

CEO of the #1 corporate sales training firm and multi-family investment company – motivational speaker, and *New York Times* best-selling author, Grant Cardone is one of America's most well-known business leaders. Much of his ongoing success is driven by being a self-declared 'factory of content' on multiple sites, grantcardone.com, his own digital network, grantcardonetv.com, and across social media. Activity which pushes people towards his multiple streams of income – which include his sales training companies, his best-selling books, his merchandise including workbooks, wrist bands, hats and clothing, his online training programmes – and has made him an in-demand speaker. With an estimated worth of

$350 million, Grant uses content to make himself omnipresent and get his message, products and offerings in front of new audiences.

What is point of content for you?

Digital is set to surpass TV, radio and newspaper. By the year 2018, people will spend more time on digital than ever before and that means there'll be more ad dollar spend on digital in comparison to TV. Attention is the name of the game – obscurity costs you money and if you can drive interest, and respond to that interest, there are no limits. For me, it's about making myself omnipresent and pushing attention towards everything I offer and all the ways I can help people. A celebrity can go on Facebook and get four million views, but the problem is he's not going to keep doing it. He's going to do it when his movie comes out. I didn't have a movie to make me a celebrity. So I am manufacturing celebrity status without the movie. I'm just using articles, blog posts, audios, videos and whatever else I can do. Everyone has to compete to get attention.

When did you start using content for your businesses and personal profile?

Around 2011, when I was 51 years old. My business was successful, I had three companies, two *New York Times* best-selling books, I was a millionaire. But I started thinking 'What can I do to 10x this?' I knew I wasn't fulfilling my true potential. I was visiting businesses one at a time and I wanted to reach and help more people. I

➜

had a drive to do and be more – that same drive that is in everyone.

You create all forms of content for your websites and social media, including your own radio and YouTube shows. Why?

Some people want to read, some people want a video snip, some people want to read a tweet, some people want to read a real article about how to be a millionaire, someone else wants to see me with my kids in a photo, someone else wants to see me flying on my private jet. All these are opportunities to connect with people via good strong content that is authentic and transparent. The totality of all that potential reach in one day is freaking insane. I've become the content factory over here so that I can get in front of all these different people who like to consume content in different forms and ways.

What is your advice for people wanting to use content?

Write an article or blog post, publish and share it. Turn that into a video. You don't need a high quality camera. I've done most of my best videos on a phone. Convert that video into a podcast or radio. Anybody can do this. You can literally stream out content or have a radio show in so many ways. ITunes makes it easy for anyone to create a podcast. Take that same article that became a video and podcast and make that a custom content for your email database – then do all of that over and over again.

People either love you or hate you – what do you say about that?

I don't care if people don't like who I am. I've never seen them in my bank, I don't see them on my plane. Haters are part of the success equation. If you are going to be successful, you will have haters and critics. If you don't have haters, you are not successful in your career. The other thing I know about haters is this: they are not talking about you, they are talking about themselves. People say to me, 'I hate you because you talk about your jet'. But they are talking about the jet they gave up on. At some point in their lives, they had the dream and fantasy to fly a private jet. They are hating on me because they gave up on it.

Finding advertisers

Advertisers just love the modern internet-connected world!

In the past they had to use print publications to reach new audiences. To some extent these were categorised in niches such as women's interest, gardening, food, etc. But because the audience couldn't interact with the advertisement, the brand wouldn't really get much feedback – they'd just hope to hit you with their message as you leafed through the publication – and many publications, even now, tend to be quite general.

So if you were a brand or business, you'd pick a number of publications that mostly fitted with what you offer, you'd pay for a load of adverts to blast the readers with and, if you were lucky, the publication might do an editorial about you too. Sometimes the adverts might be completely irrelevant to the reader in the way newspaper adverts about walk-in bathtubs and discounted magnolias in free pots are irrelevant to me.

Personally, I'd refer to this strategy as throwing a lot of spaghetti at the wall and hoping some of it sticks. This strategy is why John Wannamaker, the first advertiser to place a half page newspaper ad in 1874, went on to say 'Half the money I spend on advertising is wasted; the trouble is I don't know which half', a phrase which became one of the most frequently quoted sayings in marketing and advertising.

Well, that is not so true anymore. Not only does the internet allow for more targeted advertising; the blogosphere has broken down interest niches even further than before. Today's media is now divided into tiny specialised fragments of interest and these fragments are often led by a blogger who is trusted and has power of their audience. Even better, because clicks and sales can be monitored, advertisers can begin to see what works and what doesn't.

So, if I sell lawn seed, I don't have to engage with a gardening magazine, even though that might be a fairly good fit. I can go right to a lawn blogger who ranks top of Google for lawns and has a huge following that is obsessed with this blogger and their secrets of how to get the perfect lawn and are very vocal about telling everyone around them about how to grow the perfect lawn too. As the advertiser, I'm going to be like putty in their hands when they start telling me how totally obsessed their audience is with lawns and lawn care, and then they prove this to me through their stats and the sort of social interaction that they are getting.

The blogger might have fewer readers than a general gardening magazine, but all this blogger needs to do is tell me, the lawn seed company, about their highly targeted readers and how much their readers follow what they say and I'm in! If I then find there are twenty other bloggers also writing about lawns, grass and maintaining perfect cricket grounds, I might still decide it's better to take out twenty separate adverts with them and their targeted audiences than one big one aimed at a more general and less engaged audience.

So how do you find advertisers?

Clearly many of the income routes involve advertising for other people, whether through banner ads or sponsored posts – so where do you find these advertisers who are eager to pay to appear on your blog? Well, there are two routes – using an automated ad system or dealing direct with advertisers yourself.

Programmatic systems – aka automated advertising

In plain English, programmatic advertising (PA) is the automation of buying and selling ad space online. It allows brands to use technology to tailor messages to the right person in the right moment and the right context, and it allows website owners to get ads on their site without worrying or thinking about the sales process.

Try and think of it as a matchmaker between bloggers like you and advertisers, with the matchmaker or PA platform taking a cut of the price in return for selling your ad space and publishing ads to it.

The most popular PA platform with bloggers is Google's AdSense. It's free, easy to use, and basically does all the work for you. It scans your blog post's text for keywords and inserts a text or display ad on your website that's related to the content. So if you wrote a post about sewing, AdSense would offer your reader ads about sewing patterns and fabric companies.

Automated ads are the easiest way to build up the monetisation of your blog with very little effort. The downside is you might not like the look of the ads that appear on your blog and you wouldn't necessarily have chosen them yourself.

Going direct

Nearly all the bloggers I spoke to (even those who have managers) deal directly with the digital marketing managers at brands to get sponsored posts and, for some, their main banner ad opportunities. This means there is no middleman taking a cut and also allows bloggers to really upsell in terms of the type of opportunity they give a brand. Many people talk about this in terms of value added and offers. If you're negotiating direct, you can create custom packages by upping the fee and agreeing to do multiple posts, or a mix of content, i.e. words and video, for both your blog and social media.

Know your niche

When it comes to advertising, remember this, you're not going up against the *Mail Online* or *New York Times*, nor are you competing with the biggest websites in the world. All the bloggers that have featured in this book are doing brilliantly from proving to advertisers that they can speak to and reach a highly targeted group of people. Having a smaller audience than the huge online media behemoths is a *good* thing and one of your assets.

Open the doors for advertising

You never know who might be looking at your site, so you need to make it clear to them that you will consider advertisers using your blog. This means having an 'advertise here' button and an advertising page which ideally contains your media pack (see below). Also, if you are phoning into brands or you are out networking and meeting the marketing teams from various brands in your niche, you want to make it easy for them to visit your site at their own pace and check out what you are offering.

Having an 'advertise here' button and downloadable pack also marks you out as someone who knows what they're doing in the world of advertising. It lets advertisers know that you understand the online media landscape, the value of what you are offering and allows them to access all the information they require about your blog as well as your advertising rates.

Talking to advertisers

Remember, this is a business, and very few businesses become successful thanks to their owner sitting at home and waiting for the phone to ring. So, whereas some advertisers will approach you as your blog gains traction and they navigate their way to your 'advertise here' page, you will also have to approach advertisers (or you may have collected their details when they downloaded your media pack and, having heard nothing from them, you decide to follow up). As with business owners across the whole world, you have to get out there and talk to people, you have to be ready to network and build relationships.

Once you have made contact you need to find out who is responsible for the digital marketing or influencer budget and speak to them about your blog, your traffic and what you can offer. Then, if they haven't already downloaded it, follow up right away by sending your media pack with a friendly email recapping everything you just said.

What is a media pack?

A media pack is your sales pitch and brochure for potential advertisers. While your blog clearly shows them the visual appearance of the page their ad will sit on, your media pack tells them all the vital statistics that will convince them yours is the right blog to use.

It usually takes the form of a PDF that is either emailed to interested advertisers or can be downloaded from your blog (but it's a good idea to require them to fill in a contact form in order to download it – this helps you to generate leads you can then follow up if you wish, see 'Talking to advertisers' below).

Most bloggers have their media pack professionally designed (think of it as putting your smart professional outfit on for a meeting) and it generally contains the following information:

- Your traffic stats, monthly unique users and monthly page views.
- Your audience demographics, i.e. their age, gender, where they live, maybe their professional profile – any information that may help the advertiser identify them as valuable prospects.
- Your blog mission statement, i.e. who you feel your blog is reaching.
- Any blog accolades and awards.

- Any keywords and search phrases that your blog ranks well for.

Your media pack should also include:

- Advertising options (i.e. banner ads, sponsored posts).
- A guideline of your advertising prices.
- Any success stories from brands that have advertised with you.
- Testimonials from other advertisers.

Adblocking technology

In 2015, PageFair, which provides adblocking unlocking technology, reported adblocking cost over £15 million to publishers, which as a blogger is what you are. It is real and growing and affecting the income of blogs, especially those who rely solely on banner ads for income. As audiences get more tech savvy, and installing adblocking technology to browsers becomes easier, more and more people will be likely to pick it up. The reason they will is because people don't like adverts or feeling as though they are being sold to.

There are some ways around adblocking though, and before we conclude this chapter we will briefly outline them here.

Get your ads whitelisted by Adblock Plus

Adblock Plus provides adblocking technology and is a tool that allows its users to block ads. But through its 'acceptable ads' policy, publishers can apply to get their blogs and websites whitelisted. As Adblock say themselves: 'Since ads fuel a lot of the content we enjoy for free online, finding common ground seemed to make sense. Because we share a vision with the majority of our users that not all ads are equally annoying, the Acceptable Ads initiative was created. It allows advertisers and publishers who have agreed to make ads that abide by user-generated criteria to be whitelisted.' You will have to comply with their acceptable ad criteria. Visit adblockplus.com to find out more.

Sell your ads directly

Most adblocking technology is blocking ads published on sites by third party ad networks. You can bypass the blocking technology (for now) by selling direct and publishing your own ads as the ad images come from your own domain.

Sponsored posts

Now you understand adblocking technology, you can probably understand why sponsored posts and brand deals for on-site, exclusive content created by the blogger about the brand are such popular forms of blog monetisation and were indeed hailed as an 'adblock antidote' by the advertising industry. Because they appear as content and are designed to blend in with the blog's look and feel, not as ads, they are not affected by adblocking technology.

Look for other routes to monetisation

All of this helps cement why ads shouldn't be your only route to monetisation, and why so many bloggers employ multiple routes and offers, both directly on their site and indirectly in the real world, to earn income from their blog. Let's think back to Grant Cardone and his routes to monetising the interest he gained through the content on his blog and social media channels:

- More customers to his real world training, sales and property businesses.
- Selling online courses.
- Selling books.
- Getting highly paid speaking jobs.
- Selling merchandise.

Don't get fixated on one income source

If there is one thing we can see here about earning money from blogging it's that there are lots of routes to income and no hard and fast rules. What is also true is that blogs, particularly blogs which are led by an individual, go through shifts and changes just as our lives do. No matter what you are doing now, your goals, focus and interests will shift with time.

As such, bloggers may move through phases of getting more and less income from different sources. At various times, different income routes may appeal more than others.

If there is one person who knows about how blog income shifts with time, it is Heather B. Armstrong of *dooce* (dooce.com). Heather is widely acknowledged to be the most popular 'Mummy blogger' in the world and indeed is said to have pioneered both the trend and the business of Mummy blogging. She started

→

blogging in 2001 and has since made money from network advertising, banner ads, sponsored posts, brand deals and book deals. She is routinely estimated to have, and have had at various stages of her blogging career, a high six figure/million dollar annual income.

Dooce has twice been listed as one of the 25 best blogs in the world by *Time* magazine. *Forbes* listed *dooce* as a top 100 website for women and named Heather one of the 30 most influential women in media. She is a *New York Times* best-selling author with 1.5 million Twitter followers and an actively engaged audience. She is also a writer, a speaker and a digital marketing consultant. Now, as her children are getting older, she has begun to shift her income from sponsored posts featuring her family to consulting income for herself as a digital marketing expert.

Heather, you're one of the world's most famous and most successful bloggers and you're changing direction, tell us more!

I have made a living by taking absurdities and difficulties and frustrations and turning them on their head. But writing sponsored content was always extraordinarily difficult for me as I really wanted it to be good so that my audience could tolerate it. I always wrote about the intricacies of my life and I was honest – and that doesn't necessarily fit in so well with brands. I've seen such a shift in the requests from brands over the years. Initially, you could put a logo at the bottom of a post and that was it. Then brands said you had to mention the brand in the copy and show the product, and that was fine. Lately, it's become about manufacturing experiences with your children for the brand. My children are getting older and don't always want to take part. It's different for newer bloggers who didn't know a monetisation world before the one of manufacturing experiences.

So what's the shift that you've made?

I am still continuing to post on my website when I want to. I still have an audience and I still make money there, but I have also branched out into consulting with brands and into speaking. I've done a lot of work with Tylenol, amongst other companies, and flown as far away as New Zealand to speak.

What's your advice for brands wanting to use content or new bloggers?

Not to get too hung up on audience size. I find that it's not the size of the audience that matters, it's the engagement that does. Audiences are really different on different platforms, so you have to really find out what that audience wants from you. For me, people loved to see photos of things like my animals and my kids – they wanted me to tell funny stories about my life – you have to learn what your audience wants and learn how to give it to them.

→

What would you say to a new blogger right now wanting to build an audience?

In the beginning to get audience, you have to network, interact with people who are successful and get them to notice you. Go to industry conferences and network and meet other successful bloggers and people from brands. Just walk up to people and talk to them, build a relationship and in time they may help you by sharing your content.

PART TWO

Launching your blog, running it – and resolving early problems

Are you feeling a little overwhelmed? Don't worry! We've covered a lot – what blogging is, understanding and choosing a niche, developing a personal brand, and of course the options for monetising your blog.

These are important – these choices will help determine the success of your blog – but, ultimately, you do need to take the next step. The danger for many at this stage is that they freeze – and their great blog idea never comes to fruition. You need to start.

If you have already started a blog, what you have read so far will have given you some ideas as to how to strengthen and improve it – and what is to come will help you take it to the next level.

Chapter 6

Launching your blog

To kick off the second part of this book I want to encourage you to take real action. Yes, being clear about your niche and personal brand is crucial, but sometimes you have to take a small step while these are still not fully formed *just to get things going*.

So, get as far as you can with the decision-making and refine those ideas, but accept that you don't, won't and can never know all the answers in advance. If you spend too long procrastinating, you'll never get going. Instead my advice is to ...

... start lean! Launch with a 'Minimum Viable Product' ...

There's a great business book called *The Lean Startup* in which Eric Ries talks about the power of companies launching and testing 'minimum viable products' (MVPs). The concept is simple – you start off with something relatively basic that you can put out there to gain early momentum and get consumer reaction, knowing that you will then need to adjust and adapt it as you gain feedback from the marketplace (Ries calls it 'pivoting').

Talking about business, Ries explains how too many startups begin with an idea that they *think* people will want – and then spend months or even years in a pre-launch phase, perfecting that product and idea without ever getting it in front of their customers. Without that essential market feedback they are fumbling around in the dark – so no surprise when many discover that potential customers are uninterested and the product and business fails.

As a blogger you can easily fall into the same trap. I've seen and heard of many who try to work out exactly what their niche, audience and personal brand are before they launch, spending huge amounts of time and even money. Had they followed Ries's MPV model, they would be getting that absolutely essential feedback, be learning what's working and what's not, and be able to pivot, adapt the blog and test again and again.

Many of the successful bloggers who we are hearing from certainly did not have all their ducks in a row before they launched – the blogs they are operating today are very different to how they started out. Many of their blogs will still go through further transformation as they grow. The most important step is to actually get launched.

> Madeleine Shaw is one of the UK's best-known health and wellness bloggers. In just three years she has built up an audience of millions including 300,000 monthly visitors to her website, madeleineshaw.com, and over 220,000 followers on Instagram. She has two best-selling books, an app with over 31,000 downloads, a food range in Harrods, a monthly supper club in Fulham – and continues to create content for her hugely successful blog. BUT Madeleine did not launch with the vision she has today, in fact it was only after getting started that her goals became clearer.

What is your blog based on?

That's easy – it's based on my own experiences
that started when I moved to Australia aged 18. When
I was living there I had terrible digestive problems – but
I never thought it was linked to food. I thought I ate
healthily, but in reality I was eating lots of low fat yoghurt
and drinking gallons of diet coke. I started working in
an organic café, learned to cook and really began
to understand food – it was like a lightbulb came on.
I realised what my body needed and fell in love with
food, health and wellness. Then, when I came home to
the UK, I was on a mission to share what I had learned.

Did you have a big plan at the beginning?

At the start my plan was to be a nutritionist and I wanted
my website to be a portal to getting clients and started
posting recipes. I learned everything on YouTube, from
how to write a tweet to how to upload an image onto a
website – and I made so many mistakes like uploading
wrong images or spelling words wrong. But the great thing
about being online is that when you make a mistake, you
can change it quickly.

From the outset, I have always posted two new recipes
every week and one blog post about nutrition and
wellness. Then my readers were telling me they wanted to
know more about *me* too, so I started writing some of my
own personal thoughts and opinions.

➔

How strategic were you?

I have never focused that much on the traffic my website got, especially not at the start. The site was generating enough new clients to keep me busy, and that was what mattered initially.

I did however focus on building a mailing list by trying to get people visiting the site to give me their email. Once you have their email, you can reach someone directly in their inbox, so everyone on my email list gets an extra recipe each week. It's about giving back to those people who trust me enough and have been kind enough to allow me to contact them direct.

I've also always made sure I have consistency in terms of updating the site and sending my newsletter at the same times each week. People like to feel they can rely on you. I got more strategic in 2015. I made the decision to stop working with clients one on one and focus on reaching a larger audience through books and brand deals. It was a leap of faith but I knew I could go back to clients if I wanted to – and I'm a big believer in myself.

Tell us about your products.

I always thought that recipe books were for Jamie Oliver and big superstar chefs, not for me. But my first book was published in April 2014 and it quickly sold over 90,000 copies.

In January 2016, my Glow Guides app went live. That has been a huge learning project and has given me a few meltdowns. The app is very video based and hosts a community of people who interact with each other. I wasn't sure a community would work inside an app but it's been the biggest and most popular part of it. Then my second book came out in April 2016.

Has adding in video made a difference for you?

I started doing video in the spring of 2015 and it's definitely brought more opportunity. It has opened up doors to filming for Endemol and Mary Portas. You never know who is watching and thinking 'I like her; I want to work with her'. I don't think Endemol would have discovered me without my YouTube channel, and even if they had heard of me through my writing, they wouldn't have known what I was like on camera so wouldn't have bothered.

How is your blog monetised?

I work with brands, and I tend to do a lot of my work with them off site. I might host a dinner for a brand or film with them for their own channels. I'm careful not to have lots of sponsored Instagram posts and sponsored content on my website. People don't want to be constantly bombarded with products that they 'have to have' – they want genuine content.

What's your advice for people getting started?

People think my life is drinking mocha lattes and going out for smoothies, but it's incredibly hard work. I'm a strong believer that the more you put in, the more you get out – and remember that everyone starts from nothing.

As Madeleine has told us, there is very little that can't be tweaked and adapted on a website, especially if you have a few basic technical skills or are willing to learn through watching YouTube videos.

Photos can be swapped, themes can be altered, focuses can shift and old posts can be deleted or archived in distant corners if they no longer fit with where you are heading. Your blog is fluid and can grow and change as everything becomes clearer to you.

The only way you stand a chance of becoming a successful blogger is through actual blogging. So it's time to just get started!

Your launch checklist

What follows is necessarily detailed, but even if you don't think you're quite ready yet, do still read it *now*. As you begin to firm up your initial concept of niche, personal brand, etc., this launch process will be at the back of your mind and you will more easily identify the true moment at which to take that first big step and press 'GO'.

1. Choosing a platform and software.
2. Selecting a name for your blog.
3. Selecting a domain name for your blog site.
4. Photography.
5. Website design.
6. Initial launch content.
7. Social media.
8. Getting yourself out there.

1. Choosing a platform and content management software

This is the place on the internet where your blog will exist and where people will access it. Your choice of platform is between having your blog hosted free on an existing platform (which would leave you with a domain such as 'myblog.tumblr.com' if you were using Tumblr, for example), or creating your own platform (i.e. myblog.com) with its own content management software for your blog. There is plenty of technical information for both of these options on the internet, with brilliant demonstration videos to help, so it makes no sense trying to explain the 'how to do it' here. But I do have a preference ...

You see, you're taking blogging seriously, either for yourself or for your business, and that means you want it to look fabulous and be as versatile as possible for all your future blogging ideas. I encourage you to take the 'own domain' route with WordPress installed as a content management system.

Why WordPress? Quite simply because it is the #1 most popular content management system in the world, currently powering around 25 per cent of the websites in the entire world, and used by nearly every blogger featured in this book. I have run all my sites on WordPress – including the site for my press agency business – since 2008 and I find it easy to use and understand, and endlessly adaptable. So, this is what I recommend and what I passionately believe is the best current solution for bloggers and business owners – and indeed not only what I use for my own website but also for those of all my clients:

- Your *own* website hosting (your own piece of the world wide web where the blog actually lives and where you access it to add new content).

- Your own domain name (e.g. natashacourtenaysmith. com) which incorporates the actual title of your blog or your own name.
- WordPress software – the content management system that you will use to create, edit and manage your content.
- A WordPress theme (design) of your choice (you can choose a free template, a premium design for between $40 and $80, or pay for a custom designed site).

2. Selecting a name for your blog

Wow – this can be the toughest decision you will make! And for good reason – your blog name will define what people can expect.

It all comes down to the type of blogger you have chosen to be and the reason for your blog – are you blogging to build your own profile for entertainment, blogging for authority, blogging because of passion about a topic or blogging to become a media brand?

Let's use me as an example. I blog in the entrepreneurship and digital strategy niche – and my blog is all about my authority status, and its goal is to help generate new consulting and mentoring clients, and selling more of any digital courses I create. Now all of this influenced the very calculated decision I made when choosing to use my own name for my blog, natashacourtenaysmith.com. The personal focus is central to the blog and its aims.

Had I wanted my blog to become a media brand in its own right (within my niche, entrepreneurship and digital strategy) and featuring a range of writers, I might have called it *thedailydigital.com* or *digitalstrategydigest.com*. You see, the name conveys important upfront messages about the nature of the blog.

3. Selecting a domain name and extension for your blog site

I've already stressed that I absolutely recommend you launch your blog on your own domain, not one that comes free with whatever blog platform you are using.

You also need to select the final part carefully – .co, .biz, .org, etc. Even people who have not grown up with the internet are familiar with reading domain names and prejudging a site based on this domain extension.

Your own domain name also gives you the ability to have your own email address linked to your domain and this is key. Your own personalised email address is most definitely worthwhile and has the added advantage that, when someone sees it, they will most likely check your domain too. If you think how many emails you send a day, this is a good way of raising awareness about your blog.

123reg is the UK's largest domain registration service, managing 3.5 million of the 5.4 million domain names currently live in the UK. They recently conducted some fascinating research on how important an email address is for credibility and based this research on a hypothetical handyman's van (which they mocked up for the experiment).

They wanted to find out what potential customers thought, based on the handyman's email address, and showed their test subjects two interesting contrasting examples – handyman@ gmail.com and info@handyman.co.uk. They discovered that people thought the info@handyman.co.uk looked 33 per cent more professional and 27 per cent more trustworthy than the @gmail address.

Their survey respondents also said they were 27 per cent more likely to connect with the @handyman.co.uk owner and also thought the professional domain meant that business provided more value for money. So having your own domain name will give you an email address like this one which will in turn increase your credibility.

Increasingly, people are looking at websites, domain names and emails as proof that you exist and that you have a real space – it is about building trust and professionalism. Your own domain name isn't expensive – you can buy domain names for as little as £6.99 from companies such as 123reg.co.uk and Heart Internet (both recommended by me as they both provide excellent customer service and support at great prices).

4. Photography

One thing is absolutely certain – you can't even begin to think about launching a blog without a great set of photos. It doesn't matter what type of blog you're creating – personal, special interest, or business – they all involve you putting your face on there somewhere (if not everywhere!).

However, while the early blogging pioneers filled their websites with graphic doodles and decals of swirling flowers, those days are long gone. With today's dramatic increases in bandwidth, the great websites are all photography-led with graphic design as a supporting element. Why? Because nothing tells a great story, provides a vibrant showcase or shows exactly who you are as well as a brilliant and bold photograph.

If you want to launch a professional blog, you need a complete set of personal photos, not just a single shot. Invest in a good photographer, a decent and relevant location, and even hair, outfits and make-up. We have covered this while talking about personal branding.

5. Website design

Think of the care you might take when preparing your home for a valued and special guest. It is exactly the same with your blog site – you need to make a powerful and positive first impression *and* create an environment that is conducive to regular return visits. However, there is one crucial difference between a polite home visitor and a blog visitor – the latter can decide to turn round and walk out after only a couple of seconds with no recourse to you whatsoever.

So – website design and branding is one area where you really should be prepared to invest. It can be the make or break of your entire blogging project. I can't tell you the number of people I've met with great ideas who then go off and set up their own website on WordPress using its most basic option. You hit their site and you just know their idea is doomed – which has always ended up being the case – because it just looks amateur and not convincing. Your words, passion and expertise alone will be of little consequence if you don't have your aesthetic sorted.

So – how good are you at website design? I find that while some people are keen to DIY it, they easily become frustrated and this can lead them to giving up altogether on the blog. My advice is that if you're taking this seriously, invest in it. Pay a professional WordPress designer or developer to set it up so that it looks the part. Investing in proper branding and a decent logo says you mean business.

Designing a website will cost you anything from £100 to over £10,000 depending on what you are looking for and who is designing it for you. You can certainly find people ready to do incredibly low-cost designs but cheapest isn't always the best – you may find yourself working with someone who expects you to do absolutely everything yourself in terms of imagining and planning the site, the content and even those back-stage bits like the site navigation. You may even be left to upload photos and fixed content yourself.

In my experience most people want a lot more help than that, either for want of expertise or time. When working with my aspiring blog star or business clients, I offer a number of packages (you can find out more at natashacourtenaysmith.com/look-good-online) and ongoing maintenance and hand holding.

You'll still need to learn! Even with the most expensively designed site you will need to be able to get inside it and add things, change things and generally run the site. This means developing your own technological capabilities. But spending time learning these means you won't have to keep bothering (and paying) your designer each time you need an update. Websites are no longer static things that can be 'finished' and forgotten about. A website is never finished. It will always be evolving and changing and the more you can learn about how to do this, the more you'll feel empowered to grow your business.

You don't and can't learn a system such as WordPress overnight – but please believe me, they are *not* difficult, especially if you make a real commitment to learning and understanding them. The more you can empower yourself to adapt and update your site yourself without going back to your designer, the better.

Kat Williams is the owner of *Rock n Roll Bride* (rocknrollbride.com), one of the biggest wedding blogs in the world. Updated twice a day, the site and its accompanying print magazine attracts quirky, alternative and creative readers from all over the planet. It has won a number of awards and works with brands including Links of London, John Lewis and Thomas Cook. *Rock n Roll Bride* was born while Kat was planning her own wedding in 2008. After becoming jaded by the limited offerings of the UK wedding industry, Kat saw a niche for alternative wedding inspiration. The first edition of her print magazine, which launched in 2015, was reported by the distribution company as the fastest and best-selling debut issue of a magazine ever.

How did you get started?

Originally, my blog was about planning my own wedding. I didn't even have analytics on my site for two years as I didn't know what they were. I chose the blog name because I had black bridesmaid dresses and our wedding photographer told us we were like the rock and roll bride and groom. After our wedding, I morphed the blog into a more general alternative wedding blog and started featuring other people's weddings.

When did it become full time?

I had been working as a producer on a shopping channel and went part time in 2010, and then left completely in January 2011. My husband had told me that I wasn't allowed to quit my job until my blog was generating the same income as my job, around £30k.

→

How have you monetised the site?

Originally it was through banner ads and Google ads (we still have both on the site) although it took a lot of time to get to the point where there were enough people wanting to advertise consistently. I'd have revenue one month but not the next. Now, most of my advertisers are interested in sponsored posts, or collaborations where I might design something for them and sell it. I have a six figure income now but I don't just make money on the site. I have the magazine, I do speaking events, and I have a collaboration with a headpiece brand. All these opportunities come from the blog.

How do people find your site?

We have around 350,000 visitors a month and most of that is search traffic, people looking for things like 'black wedding dresses' or 'pink haired bride'. Search traffic is the best as people are highly engaged when the site they land on matches what they are looking for.

Social media is also huge for growing audience and traffic, but traffic from social media mostly clicks to the site and then clicks away again.

Print media is struggling – why did you decide to launch a magazine too?

You never know where the opportunity will come from. We did our first magazine in 2012 and it started as a brochure containing our best blog articles for a wedding industry event. When we published a picture of the magazine on the blog, it was as though people died

1000 deaths and our readers wanted to buy it. Even though internet is great and digital is fantastic, there's a lot of value to be seen in print and producing something physical, which is why so many bloggers are getting book deals.

What's your advice to people new to the industry?
The thing with blogging is there is a low barrier to entry – theoretically anyone can do it. But to get past that critical first six months when you are getting no one reading it and pushing through, you have to have a unique vision and something different to say – otherwise you will just be the same as everyone else. I think you need to have a unique spin on something and you have to be passionate about your topic.

6. Initial launch content

If you're close to pressing 'GO', you need content – it's the spine of your blog – and you can't launch with just one or two introductory posts either. Even though it is brand new, you want your site to look established when it launches and to have plenty for people to read and see if they arrive at your site and want to stay around. You want them to think, 'this is a great site, I must come back to it again'.

Prepare your initial launch content in two ways. First you need the content for all your general pages, such as your 'about', 'contact' and any other general information pages you might want on your site. Second you will also need content for various posts on your particular niche – and I recommend launching with at least ten posts so that those who are interested can keep finding more to scroll through. With WordPress, you can easily backdate your posts to make it look like you've been posting each week for the past few months, rather than having put everything up the day before your site goes live. Having said this, don't torture yourself trying to write the 'perfect first post' – in reality only a few people will see it (unless you have a huge social following or are a celebrity). This is just your first step in your journey, trust the system and the steps you will take – and just get launched.

We will be talking more about *what* to write in the next chapter.

7. Social media

I cover social media in Chapter 9, but people launching their blog often get confused about social media and their website. Do they need one or the other, or both? And it all takes time (yes, I know!), so how will they maintain it all?

The answer can be found by understanding the interaction between social media and your blog – and how the two drive and link to each other. So for now, let me share a story with you . . .

I was visiting Marrakech in Morocco, and spending time shopping in the medina's souk. If you've ever experienced a Moroccan market, you'll know it as a confusing, crowded, loud and busy labyrinth. People constantly push past each other and you can't see where you are going – you are looking for something in particular but you can't find it . . . or you might not even know what you are looking for until you see it.

In the medina there are paths and alleys going off in all

directions, shops inside caves, shops inside shops, shops up steps, stalls in corners, backrooms, dead ends, secret places where only those 'in the know' go. That's exactly how social media can feel – a vast and noisy complex where everyone is shouting and it seems inconceivable that anyone can actually hear or find anything.

Yet somehow, despite the crowd, noise, confusion and the lack of a definitive map, people *do* find the shopkeeper or stallholder they are looking for. They ask people, they go down dead ends and come back again, they turn a corner – and there he is, the little old man selling the glimmering babouche slippers in the exact shade of pink they were looking for. Or, if they're taking pot luck and seeing what catches their eye, they find something in the medina that calls to them, that stands out, that feels like a perfect fit, they feel they must know more about and possibly buy.

Yes, you've got it: social media is like the souk. For all the labyrinthine chaos, people do find their way through and their search and patience is always rewarded.

But the biggest reward is the peace, calm and tranquillity at the end of the search – the shop itself. There you can relax, ask questions, find out more information, have a good look at what you are buying, see a few more examples to convince you that this trader is offering you a good deal. The shop is your blog website – it's where people can step off social media and look around in a quieter space.

Now, bear with me while I take this analogy just one step further. No Moroccan salesman worth his salt simply walks around the medina shouting and shouting with no shop or stall to go to. What would be the point? But I've come across →

a few social media stars who have done the equivalent of
that – built up a large following but with no website to lead
them to, nowhere to better clarify who they are and what they
offer. Instead their lives are being taken over by maintaining
their Instagram but, with all their followers trapped there
and nowhere to take them on to, they are making no money
and feel as though they are putting in huge amounts of work
for very little return.

SO – LET'S LEAVE THE MEDINA AND RETURN TO THE BLOGGING WORLD.

Social media is where huge numbers of people are and you've
got to be in it to win it. You've got to throw your hat into the ring,
get yourself to the party, etc. – whichever cliché works for you!
It's where you can have conversations, chat and join in other conversations and make yourself known. But for those who want to
know you a bit better and see all of what you offer, you provide
your blog on your website.

This means you need both – your blog *and* social media. Social
media breaks down into multiple possible channels – Facebook,
Twitter, Pinterest, Instagram, etc. – how many should you use?
I'll be telling you more in Chapter 9.

8. Getting yourself out there

Some people set up blogs or online businesses because they want
to spend their day in their pyjamas and love the idea of making
millions from their bedroom – and some might achieve this. But

much as, when it comes to blogging, you have to be online to be considered 'alive', the best bloggers are offline too. They talk at 'real world' events, not wearing their pyjamas, they stand up as spokespeople for their niche or industry, they have launch parties, they speak at schools, they enter competitions and give presentations, they get out and about making themselves known and demonstrating their passion to real people in real life (a strange concept I know!).

It's called networking, and standing up and being counted. Even with the entire world wide web at your fingertips, the way to get your blog really noticed and give it vital monetisation momentum is not to be found entirely online. The incredible success story of Carrie Green's blog illustrates the potentially huge value of real face-to-face contact through networking.

Carrie Green is an entrepreneur who founded the Female Entrepreneur Association (femaleentrepreneurassociation.com). Through sharing the stories of successful women on her blog, she has a hugely successful website plus social media followings of over 300,000, and a membership club for female entrepreneurs which has over 3000 members from around the globe paying $30 per month (and with a waiting list for entry).

Where did you start?

I started in 2011 with a vision for creating a really cool inspiring learning platform for women in business. At the time I was running an online business offering mobile

→

phone unlocking and it felt like there was nothing inspiring available for female business owners like me. I started by buying the domain name femaleentrepreneurassociation. com and talking to other women and posting their success stories on the blog (which I still do today). It was partly because I didn't feel I was any kind of expert but I also wanted to seek out and find other female business owners like myself. The idea I might one day make money from it was not of interest to me at all. In my mind, I'd built my first business up purely for money and it had left me feeling lost and empty in my life.

What was your traffic like?

In my first month I had 387 unique visitors, in my first year I had 11,000 unique visitors and in my second year I had 80,000 unique visitors. Most of the traffic came from Google, largely because people were googling 'female entrepreneur' and those words are in my domain name. But at the time I was so busy getting my idea out there that I didn't stop and look at the traffic or worry about who was reading it. I knew I had a long way to go and I knew it was part of the adventure.

What else did you do to build your blog?

I networked like a crazy person and built momentum by taking massive action. It's too easy to take a step back and say, 'I'm putting all this work in and no one is reading it, no one is commenting'. I googled networking events to go to, found a list of them and started going along to them. I was terrified – networking is awkward and I'm a real introvert.

I've been to both great events and awful events, but I soon started to build up a group of people who knew me and knew what I was doing. People would say, 'I'm interested in your story, do you want to come and be on a discussion panel?' Then I'd say to my family and friends, 'I'm doing this thing today, come along!' I even went down to a local fair near my parents' house and a local radio station was there and I asked them to have me on the show. They agreed and it felt like a huge deal at the time – I couldn't believe I was on the radio!

And did all the effort you put in make a difference?

Yes, definitely. Through someone I met at a networking event in London, I got nominated for the Change Makers award at the MADE Festival, even though FEA wasn't making any money at that stage. At the dinner afterwards, I found myself sat next to Prince Andrew and from that, I was invited to Buckingham Palace to talk about entrepreneurship. It all came from networking, putting myself out there and forcing my idea to become a reality.

Tell us how you have monetised your blog and audience.

By 2012, I'd stopped my mobile phone unlocking business and my income had dried up, but the FEA audience was growing and I'd launched a free digital magazine. I remember having hardly any money left that Christmas, and I was panicking – I'd got myself into a strange place with money, having made it but not enjoyed making it.

→

A friend taught me how to do guided visualisations and affirmations about money in a positive way and within a week, opportunities opened up to me. I ran a couple of webinars with American influencers who had digital training products aimed at entrepreneurs. At the end of the webinar, we promoted their products and split the income. One webinar made $20,000. Even better for my blog profile, my audience was thrilled I'd brought these people to them and shared their trainings. It made me realise I could make money in a way that was aligned with what I was doing and that felt good to me.

Tell us about your membership site.

I'd always wanted a membership site and it launched in November 2013. My members get monthly training bundles from experts around the world that include things from copywriting to programming your mind for success to Facebook ads. They also get access to my community Facebook group where we share issues, set goals and chat and support each other. I have over 3000 members, some of whom have been with me from the start, and a waiting list for entry.

You're an incredible success – but I feel you didn't set out to be?

Like Steve Jobs says, 'You can't connect the dots going forward, you can only connect going back'. Looking back now, I can see the path but at the time, there wasn't a path. I was trail blazing it and there were lots of ups and downs, and all I had was my vision. But yes, I still don't

> feel like I'm an expert, more of a curator, bringing people
> together and sharing their stories to help them inspire and
> empower each other.

When you're stuck in the 'I don't knows'

So far, everyone we've talked to had at least some idea of the things we have talked about so far – their niche, what their domain name should be, who they were blogging for – about when it came to starting their blog, even if ultimately they have adjusted their direction along the way. Even in this chapter, Madeleine Shaw knew she wanted to be a nutritionist, Kat Williams knew she was passionate about and interested in wedding blogging and Carrie Green knew she wanted to launch a platform to inspire women in business.

What if you are reading this and thinking 'I don't know what I want to do or who my audience is, I just want to be a blogger'? Well, I'm going to strip the idea of the Minimum Viable Product back another level and introduce you to Carly Rowena, someone who used content creation to change her life entirely and has been taken on by Gleam Futures, the social talent agency that manage the likes of Zoella and Pixiwoo. What is fascinating about Carly's story is that she launched with no idea or grand plan. But along the way she found her direction and as a result of getting started, with none of the questions I've asked you to answer, she has ended up changing her life.

Perhaps that is why actually getting started is the most important element in all of this.

Carly Rowena is a fitness instructor and fitness vlogger who is known for her down to earth, professional and realistic approach to everything from healthy eating and fast paced workouts to product reviews and motivational advice. She only launched in 2014, but has 270,000 subscribers on YouTube, and over 800,000 views per month on her blog (carlyrowena.com) and a waiting list for clients. Yet when Carly started, she wasn't a fitness instructor and had no idea she even wanted to be one! As she says herself, vlogging and blogging changed her life.

Carly, you didn't have all the questions answered, did you, when you started out?

No! At the time, I was working for BMW as a marketing advisor. It was a great job, but I wasn't ready for that to be my whole life and I used to get really low as I had no idea what I was meant to do with my life. Then my friend asked me if I'd ever thought about doing YouTube videos. I hadn't, but I followed her advice and did some videos on embarrassing bodies and embarrassing subjects. I was so nervous that I drove an hour and a half to a deserted beach to film my first video and ended up dropping my iPhone in the sand. I was also quite into fitness at the time so did some fitness videos. Three months later, a women's magazine offered me a fitness column, which I was so excited about but I had no professional qualifications. My viewers were asking me to give them fitness advice too and train them, but I didn't feel I could offer advice. So I started doing a course to become a personal trainer while I was working full time and, as soon as I'd completed it, I quit my job and started working with clients.

When did you launch your blog?

In 2015. I had things that I wanted to talk about in longer form that I didn't want to film, and also I wanted to speak to an older audience and those who are at work in the day and can't just watch videos. What I've realised is the website and blog bring it all together. I update the website twice a week, film two videos per week and update Instagram and my other social networks every day. As soon as I wake up I post something across all social platforms straight away so people know I am alive. I go to YouTube first and reply to every single comment on my channel, and then I go to Facebook, Twitter and Instagram.

Tell us how you earn an income.

Brands started approaching me after 3–4 months on YouTube. Brands ultimately want to make a blogger's followers fall in love with them and I've worked with brands like Nike, Adidas, Women's Health, Sweaty Betty, Asda, Sainsbury's, Aldi and Urban Outfitters. It's a strange industry as there are so many different things you can be paid for and tiers of payment. I struggled with that side, but Gleam help me with all of that. I also have clients like any personal trainer but my blog and vlog helps me reach far more people. I Skype train a lot of people in India, America and Australia.

→

What's been the best thing about all of this?

Blogging and vlogging have changed my life. If I had never gone on YouTube, I never would have become a personal trainer and had the direction I do now. I only got to know and understand this world by throwing myself into it. If you have something about you, people will follow you and read what you write.

So, lots to think about! And lots to do too, but lodge all of this in your mind *now* and then it won't be a shock when you finally feel ready to launch your blog. You can even begin learning WordPress by starting a small site that you never actually promote – no one will find it so it doesn't matter what it looks like – just use it as your classroom/workshop. You won't achieve the same professional results that your actual blog requires, but you'll lose your fear and learn some useful time-saving techniques.

Remember, if you don't know the answers, don't panic about it. Sometimes the best step is to just take the first step – as Carly Rowena did – and in time, things will become clearer.

Chapter 7

Content creation

It's a new day. You're sitting at your computer, all fired up. You begin to type today's blog post – and you freeze. The screen remains depressingly blank as you feel your anxiety levels rising – you've got to write something, but what?

It's not just today. You've got to write something tomorrow, the next day and the next. But all you can do is to sit there wondering how on earth the best bloggers continually come up with content ideas. And that phrase 'Content is King' reverberates around your head, taunting you.

Don't worry, you are not alone. It's the same as the phenomenon that I remember from my days working at national newspapers. To keep the inspiration flowing we would have 'ideas' meetings, and it was the worst thing – as soon as someone asks you for ideas your mind goes completely blank.

Gradually I learned how to change my thinking to generate ideas, and to understand that any idea is better than no idea as at least then you have something to work on and develop. And that's what this chapter is about – content and how to generate it. We'll be looking at some of the theory and techniques behind ideas generation, and we'll also be examining different forms of content. You see, not all content is *written* content, and the cleverest of bloggers know how to take their written material and turn it into different genres of content, thus generating several days' worth of content from one single idea. But first ...

Get the habit!

The most valuable tip I can share – and one of the best-kept secrets in content generation – is habit. Good content comes from habit. Like exercise and healthy eating, once you're in a comfortable routine you will wonder what you ever worried about. With that in mind, let me introduce one of the UK's leading blogging experts, Sarah Arrow.

Sarah Arrow is creator of the Thirty Day Blogging Challenge and has coached over 8000 bloggers and small business owners in the 'habit' of content creation. It is a scientifically proven fact that it takes at least twenty-one days to form a new habit, and during Sarah's challenge you are encouraged to blog every day for thirty days. Having done the challenge myself, I can vouch that it unleashes your content creation habit and makes things infinitely easier.

Tell us about your thirty-day challenge

Posting for thirty consecutive days is no easy thing to do ... it's really tough at times. But content creation is like any habit – once you are into the habit it's much easier to do. It's about improving and flexing your writing muscle. Post

---

daily, and by the end of 30 days you're knackered but you have a whole body of content, and you have a brand new habit. I also advise people to blog consecutively for 30 days – most businesses and people don't have enough content to be ranked well by search engines, so this builds up a useful presence. SEO is a compound effect – you need to have one post on top of another and then more posts, so that Google builds a profile of what your site is about. If you post once a month, it will take a long time for them to understand what it's about.

What are the main problems people have with content creation?

People overcomplicate it. You just need to sit down, put your fingers to the keyboard, type and press publish. I have seen so many people agonising over what to write and the only result of that is that nothing gets written.

How often do you recommend blogging once the challenge is complete?

That's really about your audience and the type of blog site you are trying to create. For businesses, I suggest three times a week at least, ideally on a Monday, Wednesday and Friday. It's about showing up, assuring your customers that you are in business, and you want to have enough regular and recent content for them to think: 'This person or business is here all the time, they're proving themselves.' It's also about standing out and sharing your content to give the greatest chance of new incoming leads.

→

How did you get into blogging?

It was actually to save my husband's transport business. He came home one day in 2007 and said 'If we don't get any leads in, we'll be bankrupt in six weeks.' At the time I was a full-time mum. I didn't know what blogging was but I did some research and started writing 500 words, three times a week. Within three weeks the business was starting to turn around. We were being found online for specific searches and had new leads coming into the business. Before long, an international motor company offered us a contract for £1.2 million based on one blog post. My husband and I now run our own digital marketing and coaching business, Sark eMedia, and have clients around the globe.

What is good content?

What indeed? Whether content is good is entirely subjective. There is plenty online that doesn't impress me yet it has huge readership and vast followings – so really, who am I to judge?

In traditional newspaper journalism, good content is about eloquent turns of phrase and overarching themes that run throughout entire articles. It's about thought-provoking conclusions which reflect back on questions asked in the introduction. Your readers are likely to be sitting down, entirely focused on the paper, really interested in the subject of the day, and are prepared to concentrate as they read. Blogging is very different.

You see, having been a national newspaper journalist for some fifteen years, I like to think I can write. Yet I've learned that writing for the web is not at all like writing for print because a new factor comes into play, 'scannability'.

That's why in online editions of newspapers we're seeing the style changing to follow that of good blogging. An example of this is the adoption of the 'listicle' (bullet-list articles) and 'clickbait' (provocative headlines that get articles opened) genres that have successfully earned blogs readerships of millions.

So – what makes for good blog content?

Scannability is the vital component for getting readers' attention – and important for encouraging people to continue to delve into your blog on return visits. You want the blog post's general sense to be gleaned from the shortest of glances on an iPhone while hopping onto a bus, ordering a latte or scrolling through social media.

Your content also needs to be unique. An important part of this is its relevance – the way that *you* and your blog address your reader's needs. They want to be entertained, to laugh, to be educated and learn about a particular topic, to be kept up-to-date with news, or to feel like part of a community. So one hallmark of whether your content is good or not will be 'Does it meet the needs of my readers?'

And what about your own needs? The more your content meets your readers' needs the more it will meet your own needs too. Ultimately what matters most is gaining enough reach, sharing and eyeballs on the blog for you to be able to sell advertising or to engage enough people to supply your business with work.

And writing ability? It goes without saying that some of your blog will be in written form and, however passionate your readers may be, very few people tolerate bad writing for long. So we will take a closer look at this shortly, but for now ...

Content mix

Blogging industry leader and commentator Chris Garrett (chrisg.com) breaks content down into three types based on what your readers will be looking for:

1. Standard run-of-the-mill content.
2. Flagship content.
3. Pillar content.

Standard content is the material you post on a daily basis, providing simple updates, reflections of what's going on in your life or your topic, and tit bits of news and information. It's what your regular followers enjoy reading when they have a spare 20 seconds or so, just to keep themselves in the loop.

Flagship content works as the big draw to your blog. It's the principal feature that represents what your blog is all about, and the reason for its reputation. Maybe it's a single post that went viral, or a post that is considered particularly informative. It could even be a great FAQ. Think of it as the blogging equivalent of the high street flagship store, standing proudly on a busy corner, super cool and epitomising the brand to its core. Even if you wrote your flagship content two years ago, you want to promote it on your home page.

Pillar content is solid, evergreen content that gives your readers value. Pillar articles tend to be tutorial style articles of 500 words or more that give your readers practical tips or advice. They have longevity without becoming out of date, and are relevant each time a new reader discovers your blog. Readers will find these articles through search but again you can list them in a 'most popular' area on your home page. Both flagship and pillar content ensure that when people visit your blog they find something worthwhile, useful and informative *alongside* your daily musings.

So, with these points in mind – scannability, uniqueness and relevance, flagship content and pillar content – let's now examine the *two key elements* to good content creation: 1) generating ideas and 2) the actual writing of posts.

Generating ideas

Having a few tricks up your sleeve when facing the blank screen can really help unblock that creativity. Here are six that work for most bloggers:

1. Research your readers

Understanding what's going on in your readers' worlds is the key to making your blog resonate with them. There are two easy ways of doing this:

- **Use Google's keyword planner to check search volumes of specific words in your niche.** This will tell you what your potential audience is actually looking for. Research this using both short search terms (e.g. Chicken Soup) and longtail ones (such as 'What is the best ingredient for a warming winter chicken soup?'). You can also use Google's Trend tool to find out if specific keywords such as 'chicken soup' are increasing or decreasing in popularity.

Then add all the popular terms to a spreadsheet. Go through the spreadsheet and use it to generate ideas based on keywords that must appear in your blog post titles. The longtail phrases may even be good blog post titles in their own right.

- **Ask your clients/audience what they are looking for.** You can do this on social media via surveys that you send to clients/customers, creating them with online tools such as Survey Monkey. You can also directly ask people in your network what they would like to read about if you were to write on this or that topic.

2. Look at your competitors

Blogging is like any other business – it pays to keep an eye on what the competition is doing, and when you're stuck for ideas, it can serve one up on a plate! So go through other blogs in your niche and have a look at their content. Write down some of their headlines, content forms and regular articles that you love. Note any posts that have gone viral.

Now think about how you can reposition this for yourself. How can you talk about these topics in your own voice? Remember, you can take inspiration for your content from anywhere, and you may be inspired by your competitors, but ultimately your content needs to be unique for your followers (and to avoid falling foul of plagiarism!).

3. Write about what you *think* about

If you've chosen a niche that you are passionate about, you are going to have lots of ideas and knowledge in that area. You'll be thinking about your niche constantly with all sorts of thoughts flitting through your head from 'Wouldn't it be great if x' to 'I hate the way everyone thinks x'.

I guarantee you that these can generate twenty great ideas every single day that could be developed into blog post titles – all you need is to learn to spot and capture these ideas as they flit through your brain and not let them vanish as random thoughts often do. So use the notes app on your phone and really observe what you think about and the ideas that you have.

4. Write about what other people ask you

When you are an expert in your field or really passionate about something, other people will often ask you about it – and they'll either want your advice, want to hear more about what you're doing or simply be keen to hear your latest thoughts and comments. So it's simple – notice what they ask you and turn it into a blog post.

5. Hijack the news

Most niches have some kind of news websites, forums or magazines that feed people's appetite for whatever's new and buzzing. The great thing about using the news for inspiration is that you gain additional authority by appearing to be at the cutting edge of what you are talking about. We talked about this in Chapter 4 on personal branding and my key advice when it comes to using the news is to:

- Produce your own simple take on the news
- Move the news on
- Provide an alternative or opposite view to the current one.

6. Remember, no idea is truly new

Don't get stuck with the thought: 'But it's all been done before...'
So what? Content is like fashion, and all ideas come around
again. Genuinely new content ideas will be few and far between
and will probably revolve around being the first to hijack a current news topic in a particular way. It's about presenting your
unique take on things, on your own unique website and in your
own unique way.

Mark's story shows how his increasing success grew on the
back of his unique take on his niche, even (as he acknowledges)
knowing that this will occasionally be unpopular with some of
his readers.

Mark Manson is a personal development blogger
from Manhattan who blogs at markmanson.net. He
has over two million monthly readers on his blog,
social media networks and email marketing list. He
originally started blogging as a dating coach to
men, but now writes on happiness, relationships,
self-knowledge and habits. He is regularly voted
in the top fifty of personal development blogs
around the world by a number of different media
organisations.

Do you ever *not* know what to write?

When stuck procrastinating or worrying about a problem, my way is to just take the smallest first step and go ahead and do it. Usually just the act of *doing* will create more motivation and solve more problems than an hour of sitting around thinking about it. Also I try to write the first draft without any expectation in mind. That frees me to just write my thoughts without fear or inhibitions. It's afterward that I go back and decide how much potential the ideas have and whether it may be something I would want to publish (after much revision) or not.

How do you stand out?

I think it's both through my writing style and in my message. My message is very different compared to the other voices in my industry, so it helps me stand out a bit. But ultimately, the quality writing has to be there before anything else. Without quality writing, nothing else matters. I also take everything into account when constructing my brand: site design, automated emails, sign-up forms, etc. There's so much noise out there that you really need to present a cohesive and professional brand to people to really stand out, not just a couple of cool posts.

When did you start blogging?

I actually started blogging in 2007 just for fun. My roommate had a blog and said it was cool, so I started one too. I never really considered the possibility it would

➔

be read by so many people back then. It evolved over
the years, as did my goals and ambitions. I didn't get
serious about it until around 2010.

How is your income generated?

For me, almost all of my income comes from my courses
and books. But that probably has more to do with my
niche and personal preference. Blog articles and the
content I create are the bread and butter of my business
and my livelihood. If people aren't reading, then they're
not buying – and that would mean I have to go find some
other line of work. The blog posts are the engine that run
everything else.

Millions of people look to you for personal development advice. Does that feel like a huge responsibility?

It's funny – as my audience has grown, I've actually felt less
attuned to them individually. It's just that when you have
millions of readers and thousands of emails each month, it's
impossible to think in those terms. Anything you write will piss
off a few thousand people and anything you write will also
change another few thousand people's lives for the better.

If you get too caught up in pleasing everyone you'll
never accomplish anything at this level. I actually spend
a lot of my focus getting back in touch with what I care
about and what inspires *me*, then I turn around and try to
present that in a way that will help and interest others. It's
backwards from what most people assume.

Any advice for new bloggers?

It takes a lot of writing and experimentation for each person to find their own individual style and voice and to discover what they care about, what others care about and so on. This is a natural process in life, but it just so happens that when you blog you need to go through this process in a very public way which is awkward – and kind of embarrassing – but you need to be able to stomach this.

For most people, when they want to start blogging they don't realise how much embarrassment and 'I can't believe I actually published that', goes into it. So if you can't handle public embarrassment (not to mention the occasional hate email) then, as the *South Park* ski instructor once said, 'you're going to have a bad time!'. All that said, there is always room for new voices!

So, you may want to pause and collect your own thoughts about how you can generate ideas for your content. But once done, there is another equally big step to take – learning how to best *write* your blog.

How to write

When I was running my own online press agency, I wrote a fantastic training manual on how to write for national newspapers for all the graduates who joined the business as junior writers. It included all kinds of expert advice on styles, story structure, turns of phrase and so on – none of it is relevant here! Why?

The answer is because writing for a blog is fundamentally different to writing for print publications. The most successful bloggers write superbly well for their medium – but it's with devices that would never have been deemed acceptable in other genres. There's a reason for this, your audience – web users are impatient, even lazy, and don't like hanging around for long – they need quick gratification.

So, paragraphs with just one sentence? Fine. Modern grammar that breaks those hard-learned school rules? No problem if it makes your voice and the meaning come through loud and clear. It all comes down to writing for your audience – and that often means scan-readers with short attention spans.

But you still need *structure* – you can't just shove any old thing together in a chatty style – and you need professionalism, albeit in the relaxed style of the modern blog. You may even want some firm guidelines to help you get from your initial idea to the finished article, ready to post. So here are some writing tips to help you achieve this.

1. Start by drafting your blog post

You may want to follow Mark Manson's method (above) and begin by simply writing. But if you need more structure, then start by sketching out your draft blog's outline. Quickly type down your headline (see the advice box at the end of the chapter), your key points and arguments and a few bullet points of information that you want to add – and that's it, your blog post is basically there. All you have to do now is flesh out your draft, but this will usually require substantial tweaking – so follow the remaining tips below to edit and refine your first full draft into a polished post.

2. Write like you talk

Writing for your blog is not like writing an essay at college, a report for a business or an article for a journal. It is much more conversational so you need to blog pretty much as you talk. This doesn't mean abandoning grammar and punctuation – you need these to convey the natural rhythm and emphasis of your speech. But it can help to use a Dictaphone app on your phone – that way you can talk through your blog post's topic and then lightly rework the transcript to capture your natural conversational style.

3. Make your main points up top

Having 'graduated' from journalism to blogging, I'm very aware of one basic stylistic difference. Newspaper features take the reader on a journey, slowly revealing the full story or argument and often withholding the final conclusion until the end – blogs, however, get straight to the point. Their main arguments are made right away, are clear and are easy to find. Again it is because of difference in reading behaviour – online readers pay far less attention and won't give you much time at all before deciding whether your piece is worth reading or not. They need to make their decision up top, the moment they see your headline.

So think very carefully about your title, try to assess it without the benefit of knowing what it's all about – see if it is compelling and engaging, ask yourself if it clearly promises the real value of the story or is too cryptic, think whether or not you are saying something that is of interest to your readers. Remember however that most readers will scan down below the title (for a split second), so tips 4 to 8 will also help you convey the story at first glance.

4. Use lists

It's no secret that some of the most successful websites in the world from *BuzzFeed* to the *Huffington Post* churn out list post after list post – and the reason is that readers love them. Consistently I see that the posts that feature lists do the best out of all the content I produce for clients. They are quick and easy to read and can still be very engaging. So use lists and bullet points to break up text (but remember – with list posts you need a really tempting headline or title as with so many other list-based posts to choose from, you want your new readers to choose yours).

5. Use heads and subheads

Headings midway through the post are great for breaking up the text. They also provide a map of your topic, helping the reader to appraise the content at a glance, reinforcing the story that is unfolding as they read, and they help *you* to create a tight structure to your piece as well!

6. Create space

In traditional media, editors have always loved elegant sentences and paragraphs with beautiful grammar and impressive vocabulary. But online readers don't have the patience to wade through it all and are often reading in challenging circumstances (walking, on a bus, squeezed in a café chair, using a screen in bright light, etc.). So as well as keeping paragraphs and sentences short and to the point, insert big returns between paragraphs to create space on the page. This breaks up the text to make it easier to read, especially on the move.

7. Play with formatting

Another way to break down your text into digestible and readable portions is with bold and italic – it draws attention to the really important words and phrases (great for the skim-reader) and helps to keep the reader's eye moving forwards. You can also use devices like 'drop quotes' where you repeat a key phrase from the main text and give it prominent formatting such as larger font and a different colour. This can really help to keep a reader's interest simply by making the page/screen look much more interesting and inviting.

8. Break up words with images

By now, I hope, you've got the message that your readers are not necessarily all that keen on reading! So one final tip for grabbing and keeping their interest is to use images within your post. They can be directly related to the topic or a light-hearted reflection – the important contribution they make is to lure the reader and offer a more rewarding overall experience from your blog post.

Blogging isn't always about words

When we talk about blogging, we naturally think it's all about words. But in fact it's not. It's about content that increasingly takes on a number of different forms. Whereas photography, video and graphic design were once the preserve of professionals in those fields, everything is so much easier now thanks to apps. In fact, there are apps and programmes for everything from downloads to digital drawing, infographics to inspirational pretty quotes ... all of them needing much less learning or technical ability than was previously required.

So, if you have an artistic side you might be inspired by Katie Kirby's story, showing how you can combine your talent and your blogging to great effect.

Katie Kirby is the creator of *Hurrah for Gin* (hurrahforgin. com), a blog that expresses the day-to-day struggles of being a parent through Katie's hilarious sketches, which she produces using Microsoft Paint. Her site gets half a million visits a month and over 100,000 likes on Facebook, and her content regularly goes viral reaching millions. Her first book is being published in October 2016.

Tell me about how you started the blog.

I started the blog in July 2014 on a bit of a whim. I've always worked in advertising and digital and social media, but I was struggling to find work that fitted around children. I initially started just writing and posting actual photos. But there have been a couple of funny situations where I didn't have a photo, so I started drawing instead, and it quickly became apparent that people found the drawings funny.

Why do your images work so well?

There are several reasons: humour is sometimes easier and quicker to get across through pictures. Also people don't like reading big reams of text on the internet and my posts can be enjoyed instantly. My images are very simple – sometimes people tell me they are rubbish, but that attribute is all part of the humour too.

What's been the secret of your viral content?

Although I don't have to do anything to make my content go viral, I can't always predict what does or doesn't work. Sometimes I'll post something and think it isn't that great, then it goes viral. I do think, however, that it has to appeal to a big group of people. One of the most popular posts I've ever done was about the seven stages of sleep deprivation. It is a subject that affects parents for many years and everyone suffers from it. That post has had well over half a million hits. Being timely helps too. If I post something about Mother's Day on the day itself then it's more likely to go viral.

How do you monetise it?

I tried ads and sponsored posts but I didn't like them as they cluttered up the blog. Meanwhile, people were asking to buy my prints, so I started doing greeting cards. Now if I share them on Facebook, I get hundreds of orders coming through immediately. I still print and post all the cards myself, and sometimes I simply have to close the 'shop' to keep up with orders. I've also started doing research and drawing for brands, which is great as I can do even more of what I like – illustrating – without overcrowding my own blog.

Viral content

Viral content is content that spreads just like a virus through social media – and often ends up reaching mainstream media too – and it's all because something in the content made people feel compelled to *share* it. Having your content go viral is every blogger's dream as it means you reach new audiences, putting your blog under the noses of thousands of new people.

'But isn't viral content all about funny stuff like "look – no make-up!" selfies or video compilations of cats falling off furniture?' It's a good question, and it is certainly very difficult to pinpoint exactly what there is in common amongst those posts that do go viral. But, as the great book *Contagious* by Jonah Berger explains, virality isn't completely random or down to luck or magic. His studies reveal six key steps to drive people to talk about and share your content:

1. Social currency: People love talking about things that make them look good, in the know and on the pulse. So create content that makes your readers feel that way too. People enjoy the kudos of being able to 'like' or share an impressive or insightful post.

2. Triggers: This is all about the idea of 'top of mind, tip of tongue' and the things we quickly relate to because of our environments. So find out what's buzzing in your environment and use the ideas you come across as triggers.

3. Ease for emotion: Messaging with an emotional component is more likely to be shared. The more we care about a piece of information or the more we're feeling psychologically aroused, whether that is positively or negatively, the more likely we are to pass something on. So focus on feelings and get some strong emotions behind your messages.

4. Public: People look to others for guidance and have a fundamental curiosity. So if they see others reading your content, they'll look too. Go public by starting conversations about it on social media and make sure your content is easily shareable with social buttons.

5. Practical value: People love helping other people. The more usable a piece of information is, the more it will be shared. This is why discounts and voucher codes go viral so quickly. Highlighting useful tips in your content can really help to encourage virality.

6. Stories: Berger notes that good stories can survive for generations. So create content that tells a wider story and isn't just about promoting an object. Make it a *human* story – such as 'Marriage Isn't For You' by Seth Adam Smith, which was shared nearly two million times on Facebook and featured on websites from *Huffington Post* to *BuzzFeed*; or travel blogger Benny Lewis' post, 'Twenty-nine Lessons Learned in Travelling the World', which was shared more than 53,000 times on Facebook. Their topics may appear generic and conventional but they *also* offer lists of honest, relatable and thought-provoking life lessons. This type of content resonates emotionally as well as offering practical value, tied up in a good story.

What's the moral of the story?

No, this isn't my summary of these tips, but one final way to create content with the potential to go viral – and it beautifully illustrates Jonah Berger's advice too!

Content that contains a *moral* message or a greater life message that people can learn from has a huge advantage when it comes to going viral, as I witnessed with my client, Jeremy Vine.

When the BBC presenter Jeremy Vine took part in *Strictly Come Dancing* in 2015, he received online trolling (unpleasant criticism) because his dancing wasn't all that great. He then filmed a video in which he responded to one particular troll who had called his dancing 'bovine'. In the video, which he'd filmed as a simple selfie video, he talked about this troll and said that he knew perfectly well he wasn't a good dancer but would not be quitting *Strictly*. He explained his reason – as a father with two daughters under 12, he had a responsibility to show them that you don't give up on something or drop out of a challenge, just because you are not the best. Instead you keep trying to improve for as long as you possibly can, even if people are laughing at you.

We posted the video on his blog and Facebook page and within a week it had reached almost two million people, been shared thousands of times, and was being reported by journalists in papers including the *Daily Mail*, *Express* and *Sunday Times*.

Then we started hearing from teachers who were showing Jeremy's video to primary school children across the UK, and one school even started a hashtag #justlikejeremy and got an entire class to make posters about all the things they would keep trying hard at even though they weren't the best. The school then contacted their local paper which ran an article showing the children and all their pictures. It also tweeted them to Jeremy which meant we were able to publish a second post containing all the schoolchildren's artwork too.

At first, both Jeremy and I were astonished at quite how far the video went as it was certainly not slick or perfect and at one point contains the rather distracting noise of a lorry rumbling past. But looking at what Berger has discovered about viral content, we shouldn't have been surprised. Jeremy's message contains many of the elements Berger talks about, including a story, a topic that is on the tip of a great many tongues (parenting), emotional triggers and practical value too in the moral of the tale – that you don't give up just because you are not the best.

So, the show is now well and truly on the road. Your vision for your own blog, whether brand new or in need of taking to the next level, should be becoming clearer, in terms of its positioning, your positioning, where its potential lies and what to write about. But all of this knowledge does not make a successful blog. There's another key ingredient to throw into the mix, and that is traffic.

Chapter 8

Traffic jam

Traffic is one of the most important elements of a successful blog, and directing that traffic is important too. But for many new bloggers, the problem is a *lack* of traffic rather than a jam. It's like standing on a busy road – think M25 – but at three in the morning; you know what it would look like in the middle of the day, cars bumper to bumper, teetering on gridlock, but instead you wait for ages just for one passing car – and when it comes it's only your mum making sure you're OK ...

New bloggers can find their early traffic disappointingly low and slow, and this might be the case not just for weeks but for months, and even a year or so. There are exceptions – celebrities or people with a large social following ready to be funnelled to your website, or official organisations with an announcement on your blog that will make news headlines and get every journalist and interested party in the world hitting your site to find out what you are saying. Incidentally, if you *are* a celebrity whose name is searched online hundreds and thousands of times, but you *don't* have a blog to capture this interest and manage your personal profile, *why not*?!

For most bloggers, however, the reality is a flurry of interest in the first days after launch as your intrigued and loyal friends and colleagues visit your new blog but then traffic will fade away and remain low – *unless you take action.*

Traffic is big business

Large corporations spend thousands on internet marketing experts who are able to tell them how to increase their traffic – and indeed, this is exactly what I spend part of my working day doing for my clients. So getting traffic is big business – but fortunately there's no great mystery or secret to it – just content creation, strategy and hard work.

Think of traffic acquisition as a simple wash, rinse and repeat process – a never-ending cycle of publishing content, repurposing content and sharing content on social media. Alongside this you're also continuing to build a profile, make your blog findable by the search engines (based on your niche and topic), and doing what you can to make people *choose* to look you up on the internet.

The key is to embrace the fact that traffic takes a while to build – and once gained, it needs to be actively maintained. So, let's drill right down and look at the different ways that people can come across your blog.

How websites are found

In practice it's not complicated as there are only a few ways that people will discover your blog:

1. They google the actual topic or name of the blog, and yours pops up in the results.

2. They google something that is related to your blog's niche, and a relevant article from your blog pops up.
3. They stumble across it on a social media platform, either in their own feed (triggered by something similar they've previously looked at) or shared from a friend.
4. Someone else recommends it (either verbally or via the share or 'tell a friend' functions).
5. Another website recommends it or links to it.
6. They read about the website in the mainstream media or see it on TV.
7. They see an advert on Google.
8. They see an advert on their social media feed.

Now, if you think of each of these as pathways to all the different parts of the internet (or funnels – a very popular word in the online world) you need to 'reverse engineer' them to make sure it's *your* blog that people find at the end of the pathway. However, if you look back again at numbers 1–6, and then at numbers 7 and 8, see if you can spot the difference ...

That's right, numbers 1–6 are *free* traffic strategies, but numbers 7 and 8 involve paying for the adverts that generate your traffic. We will come to paid traffic strategies later but clearly the free routes are worth exploring first!

One of the main keys to free traffic strategies are your blog posts

Whether you're blogging to create an online media publication or blogging for any sort of impact, every single post you publish can have a positive impact on attracting free traffic – making your website discoverable.

So, let's look again at the six *free* routes by which people find you and how blogging increases the odds of being found for every single one of them:

1. **They google that particular website:** regular blogging increases your chances of being found and prioritised by search engines, and can especially help brand new blogs (which take a while to appear in the search results) be ranked quicker.

2. **They google something else that is related to that website's niche and a relevant article on that website appears in the search result:** remember the SEO layering impact of blogging. Blogging with carefully selected keywords that are important to your niche is absolutely essential to good search engine ranking – and using the right keywords has a compound effect.

3. **They stumble across it via content on a social media platform that they either see in their own feed or that someone else has shared:** you must share out all your own content on your own social media posts and link to your post. We'll be talking about social media in great detail in the next chapter, but think of social media as the tentacles of your brand. People gather on social media platforms in numbers so vast it's hard to get our heads around, and each post you share on social media is a tentacle reaching out into this pool of people to attract those who might be interested to hear more. You've got to be in it to win it, right, and if you are not sharing your content on social media, you're missing a potential source of traffic.

4. **Someone else recommends it (either verbally or via forwarding an email from that website that they know their friend will connect with or enjoy reading):**

Again, it's a question of letting it be known that you're in the game. It's about standing up to be counted. You must promote your own content so that people can tell others about it and you will most likely want to consider building an email list (more on this later).

5. **Another website recommends it and links to it:** If your content is good, relevant, helpful, enjoyable, engaging, funny, moving, sentimental, informative (one or all of them), other sites will link to you. You can also guest blog on other sites, at which point they will link to your own site.

6. **They read about the website in the mainstream media or see it on TV:** Journalists are always hunting for people to comment on stories, or give strong feisty opinions on whatever it is they are working on. Television channels are always looking for people to be experts or commentators. They tend to turn to social networks to find these people. If you're blogging in a niche and sharing interesting content, then journalists will be more likely to find you and you'll appeal more to them when they do find you as they will see you are the sort of person who knows what they are talking about and has a viewpoint on the subject.

So *blogging* is, in itself, a strategy for getting more traffic to your blog because it impacts on all of the above. Content creation, aka blogging, is in itself a key traffic strategy that any digital marketing consultant, myself included, would instantly put in place for any business or person wanting to raise their own profile, get more visitors to their website, demonstrate their expertise, get more customers, improve their positioning . . . There aren't many visibility problems that blogging can't help fix.

It's an opportunity to improve Google ranking, to share on

social media and get people back to the website, to start a conversation and get people back to the site, to stand up and be counted, to put yourself out there, to drive opportunity that you don't even know about yet, to nurture and grow your audience. That's why I see each piece of content as a traffic goldmine.

How much traffic do you need?

There are three main traffic strategies to consider, based on the sort and size of business you want to grow:

1. Big!

'I want millions of views and millions of people coming to my website – I want to build a multi-million-dollar empire!' OK, this means you're generally aiming to become an online media brand and make money from your blog by selling advertising and sponsored posts to brands who want to get their product in front of hundreds of thousands or even millions of eyeballs. It's all about volume of traffic – it's a viable, legitimate business model and it's the one used by those blogs that turn into online media brands in their own right, such as *The Culture Trip* (a blog started by Kris Naudts, which is now an online magazine and one stop shop for the world's best art, culture and travel).

2. Rewarding

This second route is the one that many of the bloggers in this book have taken. While they might not have multi-million-dollar media empires (although some do), they are still enjoying lucrative incomes and incredible lifestyles. Theirs is a more *personal* brand-based business, and cultivates a more intimate audience through which more niche-specific brand deals can still be made. It can bring other opportunities too such as coaching, consulting and real world work. A recent survey by Vuelio conducted in February 2016 to explore how bloggers work, their activities and the commercialisation of their work, found that bloggers who have commercialised their blog, and are blogging professionally, had over 10,000 visitors per month.

But it's important to remember that numbers and success aren't necessarily correlated.

Alice Audley is the editor of *Blogosphere* magazine, a quarterly print magazine especially for bloggers and aspirational bloggers. Every quarter, the magazine shares the best content from across the blogosphere and also offers practical advice and steps on the blogging world (it is well worth subscribing to).

She says: 'A blogger with a smaller audience, made up of an older and wealthier demographic, is going to have more financial success with people purchasing their fashion recommendations than a blogger with a huge tween audience, who don't have personal access to a debit/credit card. Luxury bloggers do particularly well through affiliate links because their audience are older, self-sufficient individuals who can take action and buy their recommendations.' We can see these forces at play with quality over quantity in Coco Hamilton's story.

Luxury fashion blogger Coco Hamilton does not compromise her personal style, tastes and preferences for the sake of a bigger audience for her blog *Coco&Co Ldn* (cococoldn.com). Despite not having a massive following, she's worked with some of the most luxury, high-end brands out there including Harrods, Harvey Nichols, Chloé and Cartier, has a six figure income and a lifestyle that will be the envy of many.

What inspired you to start your blog?

The idea to create *Coco&Co Ldn* was given to me by a friend of mine when I was working in Saudi Arabia. I'd just finished my degree studying law at Cambridge University, and had moved to Saudi Arabia to start my job as an advisor for high net-worth individuals, including the Saudi royal family. Working with foreign officials and the royal family meant that I was always exposed to the luxe market – whether it was venues, luxury brands or exhibits. So my blogging focused around a similar market. Whenever it was Ramadan time I would go to London, but when I went in 2013, I decided to put together a 'best of London' collection and start my blog. It quickly got around 1000 followers, mostly from the Saudi community, and it grew from there. Today, my audience is from the UK, Middle East and US.

Do you think you need to have huge traffic to be successful?

There are bloggers that exist who have about one to two million followers on Instagram and millions of visits to their site. I only have around 100,000 visitors per month and only around 100,000 followers across all social media. But big brands come to me so often because they know that I fit with their image – that kind of luxe, high-end style. They →

know that I cater to a very specific market of people with luxury tastes that they also cater to. The jobs I've had with brands like Cartier and Chloé are because they want to access wealthy stylish women.

Did you have a certain monetisation strategy?

I'm very focused on what I want to achieve. I wanted to earn six figures, so I worked back from there to make a plan of what to do. If you decide you want to earn £30,000 in a year, you know that you'll need to write a certain amount of posts per week and do a certain amount of sponsored features per year. You really need to understand your figures and work back from there.

Any advice for new bloggers?

I think it's important to stick to what you know. I know the luxury, international world so that's what I blog about. My blog is fully staffed, and all my team love the brands that we work with and love what we do. My followers appreciate that we are genuine.

3. Blogging for business

The last of the three traffic strategies is to generate customers for your business (which we'll be talking about in Chapter 11), whether that is yourself as the provider of a particular freelance service, or for a bigger company. And you don't need that much traffic to be successful. If, for example, you are a local business offering plumbing services, you might be run off your feet with just 60 clients per month. For business generation, traffic is not about pushing for as many numbers as possible but about your expert positioning, enabling you to grow your business to whatever size you want.

Whichever goal you have it still pays to have multiple sources of traffic. Having a website with just one source of traffic makes you as vulnerable as a business with just one customer. Increasing your overall traffic helps secure your site's long-term viability – for instance, if all your traffic comes from one social network and that social network goes out of trend, then your traffic will dry up. I know it's hard to imagine a world in which Facebook, Twitter, Instagram and Pinterest are not dominant players but we have seen social networks disappear before – look at Myspace for instance.

Email list building and traffic

Once you get into this online world, you will hear people talking about email list building everywhere – and certainly it's extremely valuable for generating both traffic and sales (although for many bloggers, their sales will come from the brands they deal with rather than directly from their audience).

The principle is simple and addresses the fundamental flaw of websites – you can monitor the quantity of visitors coming and going, but you often have no idea who they were, what interested them or how to lure them back again. Implementing email list building and email marketing solves this problem to some degree.

The idea is to encourage visitors to sign up to your email list, then you can contact them directly with updates on your latest blog posts that drive them back to your blog – this in itself helps to increase traffic to sustain and grow your blog's potential profitability – and you can make exclusive offers to them via their inbox. Of course, you'll be unlikely to get every single person who hits your blog to sign up but, managed well, your mailing list is a significant asset.

Feeling sceptical? Maybe you've signed up to one too many emailing lists and been bombarded with unwanted emails?

Well, my answer is this. The people who visit and revisit your website *are* genuinely interested in your content and they *will* want to know when there's something new to see. But unless they scroll back every time they log onto their social media, they'll miss your updates. Social media moves very fast – and what you find on it can sometimes be just too much of a lottery for a focused professional blogger.

So, while I agree that our inboxes are definitely overcrowded, we *do* open emails from sites we trust. I actively look forward to my morning emails from the likes of British Beauty Blogger for example – that is because I chose to sign up to them, I asked to be contacted and, as long as the content continues to interest me, I'll continue to open those emails and follow those links.

Mailing lists are not fool-proof. Everyone has a critical threshold when they're driven to do a complete purge, deleting all emails opened or not. But it's still an accepted and routine means of maintaining online relationships and plays a big role in growing a successful blog and maintaining traffic.

The challenge is getting that sign-up in the first place . . .

How to trigger the sign-up

Some popular bloggers and blog owners do it simply by adding a sign-up box that says 'Never miss a post' or 'Get every new post delivered to your inbox'. But for most bloggers the reality is a little harder. People have every reason to be suspicious and need to be wooed if they are to surrender their contact details.

The best way to overcome this is with what is known in the online world as an 'opt-in bribe' – usually a free gift in the form of a discount code or a useful report related to the blog's niche in order to get people to actually respond and sign up. To work, the opt-in bribe has to be absolutely compelling. Then you just need to deliver on your promise ...

Using your mailing list

The beauty of mailing lists is the degree of automation – you don't have to spend half your precious time sitting there sending out individual emails! You can subscribe to a service that automatically delivers email updates featuring latest posts to your subscribers or you can use specialist email marketing providers such as Mail Chimp, Aweber, Infusionsoft and Getdrip – these collect the email addresses and then send out your emails when you schedule it.

I recommend the latter as you have more control over what your subscribers actually receive. However, as your emails are effectively mini-newsletters you *are* having to create more content – but it is well worth the investment and plays a part in the success of some of the bloggers in this book (remember food blogger Madeleine Shaw in Chapter 6. She emails her subscribers every Thursday without fail with a bonus recipe that is not available on the website – a powerful incentive to remain on the mailing list and share content). For one of my clients, we were able to increase traffic to her website from email by 138 per cent by putting regular Thursday evening newsletters in place. That in turn directly increased sales of products from the website. So you can see how that is worth doing.

Paid traffic *vs* free traffic

Paid traffic is not likely to be high on the list of most new bloggers and I wouldn't consider it unless you have something to sell direct to your audience. It's worth knowing how it works, however, as it may be something you want in the future.

Almost every platform, from search engines such as Google and Bing to social media sites such as Facebook, Twitter and Instagram, offers you the option to pay to get your blog right in front of a targeted audience. Your blog is then highlighted on screen in the same way that adverts are. How much you actually pay depends on the platform and the competition in your niche.

However, search engines and social media operate their paid adverts in different ways.

Let me give you an illustration. Suppose I am blogging about my love of magnolias:

With a *search engine*, I am paying to appear when people type in certain specific key phrases. So I can make my blog appear instantly when someone types 'How to grow magnolia plants'. I am targeting the very close correlation between what they are searching for and what I am blogging about.

On *social platforms* such as Facebook the targeting is slightly different. Here I can target people by their age group, income, job, likes and dislikes, etc. – all the preferences that the platform has encouraged its users to specify. So for magnolias I could decide that my ideal blog audience is made up of women aged 30 and with an income above a certain level (as this increases their chances of cherishing a garden). I could also specify only users who have liked pages such as *BBC Gardeners World* page, or *Magnolia Plants Today* magazine. I can even zone down to a particular geographic area. Then Facebook will only present my ad to people who meet all these criteria.

It has to be said that paying for traffic works extremely well – when I was running my online press agency business, paid traffic was hugely important to us, making up around 40 per cent of total traffic. We only used Google, partly because I was running the business before Facebook ads became available but also because I personally like hitting people with a solution at the very moment they are googling something. It is highly targeted, and being able to offer the precise answer they want is extremely powerful. However, Google ads tend to be more expensive than Facebook ads, and there are hundreds of thousands of businesses whose success comes from really nailing down their ideal customer's identity, age, income bracket and likes and dislikes and then just being present in their customers' Facebook feeds.

Guest blogging

'If I'm supposed to put all my efforts into creating my own blog and personal brand, why would I want to post on other people's sites?'

So, guest blogging is a way of putting yourself into places where the audience is greater than your own. Many blog owners will welcome guest content because, as we have seen, the volume of content published on any site increases traffic.

Take the example of the *Huffington Post*, whose UK blogs editor we heard from earlier in this book. A large reason for its runaway success is the fact it is open for guest content. In the UK alone, some 15,000 bloggers contribute their articles to the *Huffington Post*. And it is a 'win-win' – each guest piece contributes to the *Huffington Post*'s overall traffic and each blogger is working hard to promote their own content, which increases traffic to the *Huffington Post*. And each blogger then gets the chance to use a link at the end of their piece to attract that audience of millions back to their own website.

Even better, guest blogging is a *multiple-benefit* strategy

Traffic

As with the *Huffington Post* example, appearing on websites with considerably more visitors than your own *and* resonating with their interests (i.e. your niche) gives you the chance to attract traffic back to your site. Some of these may then go on to become regular visitors, sharing with their own networks, and ultimately supporting your blogging business.

SEO and link-building

SEO is a topic that needs a book in its own right (and indeed there are plenty of great books on SEO out there) but one key element of SEO is link-building. By getting other quality websites to link back to your site, you enhance how well Google ranks your site. Every guest post you do will provide a link back to your site, improving your rankings and – hey presto – bringing you more organic traffic through search engines.

Authority in front of your own audience

If you guest post on your niche industry websites, or even news websites, you can then use their logos on your site alongside the words 'As seen on'. This association gives you more credibility in front of your own site visitors *and* enhances your personal brand (yes, everything is linked together).

Authority in your niche

Part of being a successful blogger is having an audience, but also becoming 'niche famous' to others in your niche who may then want to collaborate with you or meet up in the real world. The more you guest post on other sites in your niche, the more other bloggers in your niche will take notice of you. You might be a new blogger, but they will soon begin to think 'I keep seeing this person everywhere!'

A word of caution – it's a two-way street! Like anything in life, you can't successfully approach guest-blogging with the attitude that 'it's all about me, me, me!' Before approaching your target blogs for guest-posting, first consider the blog owner. What are the benefits to *them* of publishing your post? What can you write about that their audience will enjoy? You need to offer genuine value to the blog owner and their audience when you propose guest blogging.

Here's a useful story illustrating the benefits of approaching guest blogging realistically.

Ask the expert

Tor Refsland is a digital strategist and business coach. In his first 14 months of blogging for his business, his blog *Time Management Chef* (timemanagementchef. com) got featured on 158 blogs and websites including *Lifehack, Tiny Buddha, Inc.* and *Huffington Post*, both as a guest blogger and interviewee. That brought him traffic, enabled him to grow his email list and gave him new clients. Tor says that none of his success would have come about if he hadn't networked with influencers online and done guest blogging.

Did you have a strategy with guest posting?

I thought of it like this – There are basically only three things you need in order to succeed online in my niche as a coach: get targeted traffic, convert that traffic into a subscriber, and convert that subscriber into a customer. A guest post on the right websites can get you 30 new subscribers from the new traffic that comes your way. If I wanted to get 500 new subscribers, some of whom would most likely become coaching clients, I would have to do 17 guest posts. So I made a plan to write two guest posts a week and to start networking with blog owners and well-known bloggers who might be interested in featuring either my posts or me.

How do you connect with influencers online?

Every niche has its own influencers. These are people running successful blogs and personal brands in that particular niche. How do people normally reach out to influential people online? They ask the influencer to promote their blog post or do some crazy favour that the influential person probably wouldn't do even for their best friend. Don't be one of those nutcases. You will just burn bridges.

Connecting with people online is not rocket science. It's just like connecting with people in the real world. I have a few basic principles when it comes to connecting with influencers the right way. 1) Always provide value for the influencer 2) Expect nothing in return 3) Be polite 4) Act like a human being.

Blog owners get pitches all the time, how did you stand out?

I worked out a formula and then followed it. First of all, you start by posting comments on the blogs that you want to guest post for. Every professional blogger reads the comments posted on their own blogs, so this makes sure your name is familiar when you then suggest guest blogging.

Then you need to establish a relationship without pushing your blog contribution – send emails to the blog owners offering to help them out or telling them you enjoyed their article without asking for anything in return. Finally, you can pitch for your own post, and if you are a beginner you might need to do three pitches in order to get one accepted post.

Also remember, that the better your relationship with the blog owner is, the higher the chance that your pitch and article will get accepted. Once you start to get published on the big websites, you don't need to comment and network with the blog owner in advance. You can just pitch them right away. Your work will speak for itself.

→

What do you advise people to say in their pitch?

The pitch needs to be short and straight to the point:

Hi (First name),

I'm a long time reader of your great blog (blog name).
I would love to write a guest post for you.

Here are some suggested headlines:
– (Headline 1)
– (Headline 2)
– (Headline 3)

Do any of those work? If not, I'll get back to the drawing board.

My previous articles have been published on:
– (URL article 1)
– (URL article 2)
– (URL article 3)

Let me know what you think.

Best,
(Your first name)
(Your blog's URL)

The concept of 'guest blogging', writing or contributing content to other websites that already have more visitors than your own, may seem perverse at first glance. But rather than seeing it as feeding the competition, you should instead view it as benefiting from the greater profile of other sites – it's just like using social media, just another way to engage with the online audience at large and attract links and traffic back to your own site, as well as enhance your personal brand by showcasing you on bigger sites.

Other traffic enhancers to consider

Search Engine Optimisation

SEO intimidates a lot of people, but read on ...

As we are seeing, many of the elements we are talking about in this book are inextricably intertwined and, done separately *and* together, increase the visibility of a blog. For instance, blog posting itself is an SEO strategy that will increase traffic – similarly, good SEO throughout your site as a whole will also increase traffic. Likewise, guest blogging will bring you traffic from other websites whilst also improving your own search engine rankings by increasing links to your site.

So, don't worry if you're feeling that SEO is too complicated to bother with – as soon as you start blogging and building up your site, you're already making it SEO-friendly! Just keep on creating original content, using social media, commenting on other people's posts and guest blogging.

But there are also things you can do to strategically improve your SEO rating:

- **Keyword optimisation**: This means first researching the words and phrases that potential readers might be using in their searches (reflecting their particular interests) and then creating blog posts that match these keywords. It's a skilled process, with best practice being to use just one target keyword per blog, and to make sure that keyword is visible in your content, subheadings, blog title and URL so that search engines can clearly identify the keyword or phrase.

- **Google Search Console:** This is one of those useful Google tools and it monitors your site for the kind of things that search engines *don't* like – things like broken links, error messages and any other crawl errors. You can then put these right.

  You can also use the tool to reveal what Google actually 'sees' on your site and uses to assess its relevance to a search. So, particularly with an image-led site, it will tell you if it isn't getting enough information to decide if your site is relevant or not.

- **Install a SEO plugin:** WordPress in particular has numerous free SEO plugins that will help with SEO. They're really easy to use and will give your blog those extra tweaks so that search engines can find you more easily.

Getting your blog noted and written about by 'lists' in your niche

Across the blogosphere, there are all sorts of organisations ranking bloggers, and blogs, and publishing posts, complete with links, about blogs or blog stars worth following and reading. Such content is published both by large organisations such as Vuelio, who provide a PR database to connect PR professionals with media outlets (including bloggers), online magazines and even other bloggers themselves. You'll see these online articles with headlines such as '10 beauty bloggers to follow in 2016' or 'The top 10 UK beauty bloggers'.

These lists have a two-fold benefit. First, they add a dose of credibility as you're able to say 'As seen on this top 10 list' and secondly, if they're being published by larger sites, you benefit from some of that site's traffic.

Part of being featured on these lists is down to being chosen, but the rest of it is about the quality of your blog and social media traffic and, crucially, making yourself known to the list compilers, as Paul Miller from Vuelio explains.

Ask the expert

The Vuelio media database helps to connect PRs and communications professionals with media professionals. Once the database was all print and broadcast journalists, but as the media has changed and fragmented, Vuelio has added bloggers. Their weekly publication of the Top 10 UK bloggers for myriad categories is simply a matter of checking the most influential names in the database. Today, all bloggers aspire to feature in Vuelio's lists as it brings huge amounts of credibility, clout and helps them stand out, all part of building a strong personal brand.

How do you decide who gets to feature on your Top Ten list?
We run a complicated algorithm that assesses bloggers on all sorts of factors and indicators as to their success and influence. This includes web traffic stats – it's a proprietary algorithm, so I can't provide exact details, but the individual ingredients are not too surprising. We have a number of sources for web traffic and social signals are also a big part of it – for example, activity, engagement and following across various networks – and we also calibrate to reflect the importance of certain networks to a particular blogging niche. For instance, in a highly visual fashion niche such as fashion, Instagram might have higher weighting than other networks. From this, and other information, our algorithm scores bloggers.

→

Why do so many bloggers aspire to be noticed by Vuelio?
It's partly because we link to them from our site and so send them lots of traffic. But also, it helps in their conversations with brands because it gives them a stamp of approval and an official status. From the point of view of PRs and brand representatives, seeing a blogger on a Vuelio list makes that blogger more likely to be someone they will work with.

How can a blogger get on your list?
Firstly, we need to know who you are. We need to list you as a media professional in our database. We have a team of researchers who are using lots of clever search technology and tracking technology to see new websites and new bloggers, but increasingly bloggers come to us before we find them. If we don't know about you, tell us! Get in touch and introduce yourself.

Publicity

With my own clients I use both online and real world techniques to increase their visibility, profile and traffic. The real world techniques are mostly to do with publicity, ideally getting the client on TV or in a magazine or newspaper.

The impact of appearing in the media is threefold: firstly, people are more likely to Google you or follow you on social media; secondly, media exposure enhances your personal brand; and thirdly, being able to add a stamp such as 'As seen on BBC 1' or 'As seen in the *Sunday Times*' adds valuable credibility to your blog, thus further engaging your existing website traffic and any new arrivals to your site.

Chapter 9

Getting social

Using social media simply means communicating on the internet through 'social' platforms such as Facebook, Twitter, Instagram, YouTube and LinkedIn. The chances are you already use social media – along with one third of the entire world. You may also know first-hand how it can help you in your professional life, especially if you're trying to build a business.

Today, vast numbers of people use social media instead of search engines like Google to find whatever they're looking for. Given that engaged audiences are the key to a blogger's success, social platforms help you to grow your reach, influence and engagement beyond just the traffic that reaches your blog itself.

However, it's not just about funnelling traffic. Using social media as a blogger is about getting attention, networking, generating opportunity, keeping your audience engaged, having conversations, building loyalty, building a personal brand, being helpful and making new contacts.

Let's be clear about the benefits of social media

That means dispelling the most common myth ...

'Social media's GREAT! It's easy marketing – and it's FREE!'

Woah – slow down. Many brands spend significant parts of their marketing budgets on mastering social media and engaging their customers on it. This tells you something about making social media work. But there's more – there's the *time* you will need to commit to it, and the *time* creating new content or repurposing old content. As Grace Bonney tells us, it can feel like a LOT of extra work (but as she also tells us, it pays off).

Grace Bonney is the founder of *Design*Sponge* (designsponge.com), and has been declared a 'Martha Stewart for Millennials' by the *New York Times*. *Design*Sponge* attracts over one million readers a day. Originally an interiors journalist, Grace started her blog as a hobby before realising she could turn it into a career. Grace has been a featured guest on *Good Morning America*, *The Nate Berkus Show*, *The Martha Stewart Show*, *Martha Stewart Radio Show*, NBC's *The Chew* and has been a keynote speaker with a wide variety of organisations ranging from design schools and trade organisations to design guilds and national corporations. In 2009, Grace published the first *Design*Sponge* book, which now has over 100,000 copies in print. Her new book, *In the Company of Women*, is out now.

You have HUGE social followings across four different social platforms, how important is social media to the success of the site?

Social media support is crucial, not just for the site but as another arm of the *Design*Sponge* brand. I think of the brand as a hand – each finger (social, the blog, events, books) is important and vital to the success of the company's overall strength. Being present on several of those platforms in the early days was hugely instrumental in building larger numbers of followers. I wasn't doing that consciously, but I think being an early adopter is always the quickest way to dig your feet in and build a solid foundation.

How do you manage the work involved in creating content for all the social platforms that you're on?

At first it felt like a ton of extra work and, honestly, it still does sometimes. It can feel like you're being expected to provide high-quality, original and FREE content for yet another platform and to re-prove yourself over and over again to new audiences. That's true to some degree. But what I learned (primarily through falling in love with Instagram) was that it was also a chance for me to recharge, reconnect with and rediscover what I first loved about the creative community. Each platform brings a totally new group of people (and often a much younger generation of people) who can both inspire and be inspired by these new connections.

→

You started *Design*Sponge* as a hobby, did you have any major plans in the beginning?

Never. I always thought (hoped, really) that blogging would be, at best, a modern way for me to get my foot in the door at a magazine one day. That was my dream job. I finally got to work for my favourite magazines but slowly they all closed. *Design*Sponge* was really coming into its own around that same time (2007/2008) and I realised that if I worked hard and focused on the business part of my site, I could really build something special that could support me and the people I love and work with. I'm proud to still be running a profitable site over a decade later that has stayed true to its core ethics and mission since day one.

In terms of the monetisation of the site, which routes have been most successful for you and are there any that haven't worked out?

In the early days we were able to sit back and field ad requests and be INCREDIBLY picky about what we did and didn't take. I cringe thinking about some of the emails I sent people, rejecting their ads for not being as aesthetically in line with our site's look as I'd like. But as blogging has gone on, ads are no longer something people tune out or just get used to – they actually expect to see them. So sponsored posts have become the norm, as well as bloggers being brand ambassadors for outside companies. We do a mix of all these methods as well as writing books that we hope will add value to our readers and the company as a whole. But when it comes down to it, without plain old ads and sponsored posts, we wouldn't be able to pay our writers the way we do. I don't love doing sponsored content (we're very selective about what we run, how often and how it's handled) but those bigger budgets mean our team members are paid well and our full-time employees have good health insurance. A happy, well-supported team = a good site.

The site has brought you tremendous off site opportunities too, such as your best-selling book. When you look back over the past ten years, what have been the most amazing/stand-out highs that *Design*Sponge* has brought you offline?

The opportunity to create, produce and (soon) promote my new book, *In the Company of Women*, is the greatest experience I've had working with *Design*Sponge* over the past 12 years. Over the past few years, I realised that my interests were shifting from the objects and designs themselves to the people behind them. Those real life stories felt more inspiring and relatable and led me to move the site away from so much product-based consumerism to talking more about people, their lives and what makes a house feel like a home (which often has more to do with feelings, family and DIY). This new book gave me the chance to meet over 100 of my biggest idols (all women running their own creative businesses) in person and ask them questions I've wanted to ask for years. I have never been as proud of a project I've done before.

So, the benefits of being all over social media far outweigh the time cost, and here's why

1. **You'll reach new audiences:** You will never *ever* have as many visitors to your blog or website as you do to your social media platforms each day. Joining the social media circuit is like going fishing in a pond absolutely stuffed with fish and, best of all, the fish are choosing to come to your hook – you don't have to try to catch them. It's like holding out a beacon that showcases who you are and what you offer. This is especially the case when you use hashtags (#) to give context and searchability to what you are saying (more on this below). It's not just about people coming to you – you can join in with relevant discussions that are already happening and that way introduce yourself to a whole new group of people.

2. **You can get in front of people who are time-starved:** We live in a busy world. We may be interested in your topic but we don't necessarily have the time to read every post you publish or keep returning to your website. So, chat in brief about your topic on social media as well as sharing your blog posts, and those who don't necessarily have the time to look through every post on your blog will still become aware of who you are and what you are talking about.

3. **You can interact with your own audience and existing readers:** Social media isn't just about reaching new people – it's also an easy and casual way to stay in touch with those who already know you. If you are blogging for your business, I would look out for existing customers on social networks and use tools such as 'Twitter lists' to

group your existing customers onto a private list. If you continue engaging with them, this will help them come back to you as repeat customers and remind them to recommend you.

4. **You can increase your likeability factor:** Social channels often feel more personal and fun than websites and are a great way for audiences to quickly size up the personality of a blogger or a business.

5. **You can network with influencers directly:** Most people do their own social content, especially those on Twitter. All of my well-known celebrity clients are responsible for their own tweets. This means if someone tweets them, they do usually see it (unless they receive a particularly high volume of tweets that makes it impossible to scroll through everything). Now think about your blog, and just how powerful it would be to connect directly with whoever is most influential or who you most admire in your niche. No secretaries guarding the gates to their ivory towers or web managers manning their inboxes. What you do with these connections is up to you, but it might be that they end up sharing your content, inviting you to an event, letting you guest blog on their website ... However, consider this fact: 91 per cent of mentions on Twitter are made by users with fewer than 500 followers so interacting with 'normal folk' is just as valuable if you want people to talk about you.

6. **You'll get better partnerships with brands:** Brands increasingly look across the whole digital landscape to determine who to work with. To increase their prices, savvy bloggers offer mixed packages to brands, including a number of blog posts shared across social media and social-only posts too.

7. **It will enhance your personal brand:** Vuelio, one of the large authoritative organisations that rank bloggers, have already told us directly that they use social following and engagement as a factor when they rank the best bloggers in the UK. Likewise, being visible on social media helps you to generally enhance your personal brand.

Can using social media improve your search engine rankings?

There have been mixed messages from Google about whether or not social media is considered in their ranking algorithms, although Bing has stated clearly that social media does contribute to ranking in search engines (over time) through influence and being influential.

However, most digital marketers, including myself, consider it highly unlikely that Google is dismissing social signals altogether, especially as Google has also stated that social networks should not be looked at for their short-term benefits, but rather a long-term play.

Certain things are clear about the way that social media benefits rankings.

For a start, if you have social media profiles, they do tend to rank on page one of search results for your name, or the name of your blog or business, and so allow you to fill Google results with your own brand. This suggests that Google does watch who gets good social signals and shares day-in day-out and as such may increase their rankings over the long term.

Also, increased social media exposure and consequent

growth in visitors to your site increases the chances that other websites will link to your content, which definitely improves your overall ranking position.

We have heard from Vuelio and others that they *do* look at bloggers' social media engagement and followings to determine who makes it into their top bloggers list. Inbound links from large authoritative sites like Vuelio that carry huge clout in Google's eyes will also improve your overall rankings.

Which social networks should you be on?

The main social networks are Facebook, Instagram, YouTube, Twitter, LinkedIn and Pinterest, with new networks such as Snapchat gaining huge traction. Each is slightly different and requires different types of content to really work effectively – no wonder then that social newbies can feel completely overwhelmed about the content they need to create! So let me try to reassure you . . .

I'm going to first provide a brief outline of the main social platforms, and then tell you about the rule I use to prevent social overwhelm.

Facebook *Strengths:* • World's largest social media platform • Ideal for conversations and relationships • Most powerful traffic driver	You're probably already on it personally, so using it professionally (through business pages and groups) can be an easy step. Facebook is ideal for conversation and building relationships, and great content can result in huge reach as it gets shared by other users. It's the largest social network in the world with 1.4 billion users, a quarter of whom check their account five times a day, and research shows it drives the highest amount of referrals and traffic to websites than any other social network.
Twitter *Strengths:* • Great for topical trends • Good commentator platform for gaining authority • High visibility for media opportunities	23 per cent of adult internet users are on Twitter. It's brilliant for riding topical trends, joining or creating discussions and sharing content. I think of it as a 'commentators' platform' tool – it can be really helpful for establishing authority and expert status. Twitter is used widely by the media, so can also be a way to raise your own profile through connecting with journalists and commenting and sharing content on topical issues in your niche, increasing your chances of being asked to be featured by the press. Most of my media opportunities, such as being asked to be a guest on radio, have ultimately come via Twitter. Customers will also use Twitter as your company customer service line, which lazy brands find out to their detriment once users start complaining!

Instagram *Strengths:* • Growing fast • Perfect for visual content	Instagram is growing fast and with 300 million accounts has more members than Twitter. It's about telling the story of what you do visually and is excellent for anyone with a visual story, i.e. bloggers and business owners in fashion, food, art, lifestyle niches, etc.
YouTube *Strengths:* • Leading video platform • Second largest search engine	The king of video content and the world's second largest search engine. Quality is going up on YouTube though, with many bloggers producing videos that are like mini programmes in their own right, nicely filmed, with great sound and opening and closing credits. Selfie videos filmed with bad light via laptop cameras no longer cut it.
Pinterest *Strengths:* • Focus on female and food content • Second largest social network referring on to websites	Pinterest is the second biggest of all social networks for referring traffic on to websites, and more than 69 per cent of users are women. It's another visual network and particularly popular with food bloggers with over half of users discussing food-based content.
LinkedIn *Strengths:* • The platform for B2B professionals • Easy for posting links to your blog	If you are any sort of expert or blogging for business to business purposes, LinkedIn is all about your professional profile. You can either post links to your blog post on your news feed or upload your blog direct to LinkedIn. ➔

Snapchat	Snapchat completely isolates itself from the 'social' aspect of social media in that it is a scroll-free, comment-free, share-free, hashtag-free zone. Despite this, it is one of the most engaging platforms. It allows you to market yourself through a completely unfiltered, un-edited and instantaneous lens. It allows you to project real-time updates of your life to your followers, giving them the authenticity that platforms like Instagram have completely removed. Plus, the 'disappearing picture' concept always keeps them wanting more!
Strengths: • Unique and fresh concept – real-time only with no scrollable history	

Confused? I hope not as the different strengths should already be drawing you to one or two platforms. But to make your final choice I recommend my **2 × 2 × 2 Rule.** Ask yourself the following two questions, then choose four social networks – two to prioritise and really work on, and two to maintain.

First, the two important questions

Question 1. Which networks do my target audience use?

This is all about where your audience is and how you want to monetise your blog. You need to focus on platforms where you can reach your audience, engage with them and have true impact.

So – if you want to build a consumer-facing blog and make money through brand deals, then Facebook and Instagram are good but LinkedIn is not so good. If you are blogging for yourself as a solo service provider such as a tree surgeon, then you want to reach regular people who have houses with trees *including* those who haven't yet thought about pruning their trees. I'd say you'll find them on Facebook. If you are blogging for your business that sells business to business services, then go for LinkedIn.

Question 2. Which networks best match my ability to create content?

Just as you can all too easily go mad with content and end up overwhelming your audience, so you can quickly lose steam and watch your social media accounts dying a slow painful death. I don't know about you, but if I arrive at a feed and see it hasn't been updated for a few weeks, months or in some cases (and this is true with some of my clients even though they run large businesses) years, I immediately think they must have given up and gone out of business.

So you're looking for social platforms that feel easy and natural to you – and that means content creation that you are competent with and can maintain. Hence for many people YouTube is not a great starter option – it involves technical skills and equipment for high quality video editing. Now choose your 2 × 2 – think 'Main and Maintain'. You need to focus on just two platforms as your *main* platforms and really throw your heart and soul into content and engagement. Be there every day by sharing scheduled posts, promoting other people's content that fits with your overall message and either answering questions or joining in conversations that are relevant to you.

Then you select another two platforms which you *maintain* by posting occasional updates (i.e. once a week so as not to look as though your business is fading away).

This gives you a presence across four platforms but without all of them taking over your life.

How to get more followers

Everyone wants more followers because, quite simply, the bigger your audience the more visitors you'll get to your site – and the more reach you have across social platforms the more you communicate whatever it is you are selling, from brand deals to your services as a dog walker.

But what really matters here is an *engaged* and *real* audience. Anyone can go out and buy 1000 followers or 10,000 followers but if, in fact, they are 'fake followers' who are not interested in you or your service, what's the point? For example, if you visit a blog with 10,000 followers but no comments on the posts, you are likely to assume they have fake followers (well, I do, anyway). This undermines the credibility of the blog and puts off potential new followers.

So here are some proven ways to use social media to generate authentic and valuable followers.

Create content

Yes, so content creation itself is not only a strategy for traffic, it's also a strategy for social followers. For some of your social media content you'll simply be posting the URL of your latest blog post. However, social networks also require their own content created specifically for that platform. It's worth it – 'Interesting content' is one of the top three reasons people follow people on social media, and if your content attracts the right followers to you it gets shared and in turn leads to more followers.

Social media content is short and, depending on your chosen platforms, often visual. So use tools such as Canva and apps such as Wordswag that make it really easy for you to create beautiful graphics and quotation images.

Use hashtags

A hashtag – the # sign – turns any word or phrase into a searchable link that pulls together all content also containing that phrase, and hashtags make social media sites easily searchable. In my field, I use hashtags like #digitalmarketing #webdesign #visibility because that means anyone wondering about those topics can then find my content. I also use hashtags that relate to the types of clients I know I can bring really value to such as #tvpresenter or #entrepreneur.

One of my clients is an IVF clinic and we use a range of fertility, IVF and pregnancy related hashtags (dozens at a time on Instagram). Hashtags allow our content to be found and rapidly increase our following, but most importantly they only bring followers who are genuinely interested in what we are offering – valuable followers:

#pregnancy #pregnancyproblems #pregnancytest
#ivf #ivfjourney #ivfsuccess #ivfbaby #ivffail #ivfsupport
#ivfjourney #ivfsuccess #ivfcommunity #fertility #fertilitydiet
#fertilityawareness #fertilitytreatment #naturalfertility
#conception #preconception #baby #babies #ttcsisters
#ttccommunity #ttc #ttcsister #bfp #miscarriage
#miscarriageawareness #infertility #infertilityawareness
#rainbowbaby

However, we don't just pick these hashtags out of thin air. We do extensive research to identify the best hashtags for people on the particular networks we're on, and people who might benefit from the services this particular clinic provides. This gives us the list of hashtags that go onto every Instagram post we publish – and we may add even more depending on the particular topic of the individual post.

Doing your hashtag research is crucial. Without it I would certainly never have learned about the hugely popular hashtags #ttc (trying to conceive) or #ttcsister (trying to conceive sister – suggesting a supportive and community element to the hashtag) or #rainbowbaby (like a rainbow after a storm, a rainbow baby comes after events like a miscarriage). But as a result of this hashtag research relating to our regular content we have grown our Instagram following by 300 per cent in just four months.

Join in conversations

Like so many people, I made the mistake in the beginning of just shouting out on social media – simply posting links to my blogs and occasionally commenting on something topical, and then wondering why nothing was happening and no one else was saying something.

Remember, as with everything else to do with blogging, building an engaged audience takes time and one way you must do this is by participating in other people's conversations. They have established the audience, you simply join in with something interesting and relevant to say.

When you are new and not well known and people aren't automatically responding to you, then you respond to them! Just scroll through your social feeds for relevant conversations and join in. The great thing about social media is you don't need permission to join in – you can just do it!

Be topical

I've said it before: *the news is the gift that just keeps giving.* And I'm talking about both mainstream general news and your industry news. So if you aren't sure what to say, then talk about whatever is topical – events in the wider world and/or things in your niche or business industry. The best thing about talking about niche or industry specific news is that it makes you look totally on the ball, helping present your opinion as part of your identity, your personal brand.

Social media as a minimum viable product

Earlier in this book, I talked about MVPs – minimum viable products – and the importance of accepting that you can't have all the answers in advance and sometimes you just have to get started. Social media can in itself be an MVP, a way of getting launched and getting started before getting your website and photography in place, especially if you are trying to start on a budget.

However, I categorically don't recommend building your business on social media alone, because social media platforms are ultimately owned by someone else and their popularity can change. Facebook is currently the largest platform in the world BUT there is a whole anecdotal movement of young people apparently not using Facebook as they don't want to be on the same social platform as their parents.

It's not just about their popularity either, as social platforms can also make subtle shifts in how they operate which can affect your reach. Ultimately, to be really credible you will need to have a website – we've heard time and time again from all our stars in this book that your website is something you own, it's the spine of everything you do and the heart of your brand.

To see how starting with social media can work for some people, take a moment to read Emma Mumford's story.

Emma Mumford aka 'The Coupon Queen' built her audience initially on Facebook with her page *Extreme Couponing and Deals UK*. Within a year, she built up 100,000 followers, which she turned into an online business. She now also runs lifestyle blog *The Coupon Queen* (excoupuk.com/blog), which is also monetised.

Tell us how you got started.

All of it evolved from a personal hobby of couponing and saving money to get myself out of £7000 debt. My friends pressured me to start a Facebook page to share the knowledge I'd gained, so I set one up in 2013 and called it *Extreme Couponing and Deals UK*. Then in 2014, I set up the website for *Extreme Couponing*. It was then that brands started getting in touch with me and asking me to review their products and feature their deals and coupons. I then realised I didn't just want to do money saving, I wanted to review beauty and fashion products too. So I set up my own blog as *The Coupon Queen* – that was the name I'd been given by the press and it had stuck.

How did doing it all 'the wrong way around' help?

It made it easier for the blog and business to gain traction as I was able to share my posts to the audience I already had. And it made it easier to get brand deals for my blog – because I already had an engaged audience.

How are your blogs monetised?

Both websites use affiliates, but *Extreme Couponing* uses more. Blog wise, it's monetised through sponsored posts and AdSense, same with YouTube and the same can be said for *Extreme Couponing*.

You must know a lot about social media?

What I have learned is *don't ever get comfortable*, and don't ever think that once you've learned something it will still be applicable in six months' time. Social media is constantly changing, especially Facebook.

So social media isn't an exact science?

It's definitely not and there is no secret solution. I have been doing it for three years and what I was doing on day one is so different to what I am doing now. Also, it's important to do social media even when you don't fully understand it. I do Snapchat, which I don't really like but it gets me blog views. I didn't understand Instagram initially, but I've turned it into an extension of my blog. It's all about really optimising the channel as such and tailoring it to get visitors to your blog as that enables opportunities.

So which social media channels do you prefer to use?

For me, Facebook has been the best from a business perspective – but for my lifestyle blog Instagram works the best. I think it really depends on the topic of the blog and where your followers are based. I started vlogging in 2014, which was a huge step for me, but because I had the audience already my videos started getting views quickly.

Social talent

Inspired by the huge social audiences that some individuals have, a brand new industry was pioneered in London – managing and monetising 'social talent'. The phrase was coined by Dominic Smales, the founder of Gleam Futures, an agency that manages the UK's, and now America's, leading digital talent including Zoella.

As Gleam themselves say: 'We live in a world driven by clicks, follows, likes and comments. It's by these metrics of engagement that we measure success. We only manage quality talent who are among the top social creators in the world, dedicated and passionate individuals who are determined to be professional and accountable while exploring their potential in all areas of media and merchandising.'

Gleam's founder Dominic has publicly stated: 'TV agents would laugh, but in two years' time it's going to be a different landscape. YouTube talent will be way more influential.' Perhaps it's not surprising then that celebrities from more traditional media have started getting in touch to ask how they too can create relationships with online audiences the size of some of Gleam's stars, which is far more than even Saturday night TV can deliver.

Most of Gleam's stars have huge followings and engagement across multiple platforms from their blog to social media. Take Zoella, who started her blog and YouTube channel in 2009 to share her love of all things beauty and fashion with the online world. She has 7.6 million monthly visitors to her blog, ten million subscribers, 49 million monthly views on YouTube, 4.13 million followers on

Twitter, 7.1 million on Instagram and 2.55 million likes on Facebook.

When you consider that flagship programmes on television such as the 2015 *Strictly Come Dancing* Final pulled in just 11.9 million viewers, you can see how huge the likes of Zoella's reach is! She is thought to earn over £50,000 per month and has just recently bought a £1 million house in Brighton. It is not surprising given the size of her audience that brands queue up to work with her and her income comes from a wide variety of sources including on-site adverts, YouTube, brand sponsorship deals, product placements, her book, beauty range and even a tour.

Just as celebrities have talent managers who manage and build the work side of their lives, so Gleam does that for the new celebrity digital stars. We're going to finish the chapter by meeting Lily Pebbles, one of Gleam's stars. You will see that it is the sheer effort and consistency Lily put into her blog and subsequently vlog on YouTube that has led to the success she enjoys today.

Beauty and lifestyle blogger and vlogger, London girl Lily Pebbles has a creative eye for photography and a salon-worthy nail polish collection. A self-taught beauty expert, Lily posts on her website, lilypebbles.co.uk, most days, and uploads two YouTube videos a week, focusing on a refreshing mix of beauty, style and city →

life. She has 350,000 subscribers on YouTube, and two million monthly views. Her blog gets over 500,000 visitors a month, and she has a following of over 120,000 on Twitter, 100,000 on Facebook and 320,000 on Instagram.

How did you get started?

I started my blog in 2010 when I was at Birmingham City University studying marketing, advertising and PR. In our third year we had a digital marketing module in which our teacher encouraged us all to start a blog and a Twitter account. My first blog post was based on what I had received for Christmas, and I called it 'What I Heart Today'. Once I left university, I saw the blog as an added benefit that might help me get a job. When I was interviewing for jobs, people were really interested that I had this blog. It shows you have a passion, creativity, can focus and write, and that you are being proactive.

Did it take off straight away?

Absolutely not. I wasn't even doing it properly and posting every day until around two years after I left university, by which point I was working in marketing for a beauty brand. Because I was holding down a job, I did most of my blogging on a Sunday and in the evenings. I'd take photos and write the text for six blog posts at a time and schedule them to publish during the week. By 2013, I'd started making a bit of money from Google ads and attending events with other bloggers and I knew I couldn't carry on doing both the blog and working full time. I was living at home with my parents and I knew that

if there was ever a time to do it, it was then. So I quit my
job in November 2013 and gave myself three months to
start earning a decent London salary from the blog.

How quickly did things change?

As soon as I had the 24/7 hours to put into that blog,
everything changed and my stats went up. The quality
of my posts changed, I could work with daylight hours, I
could take better photos and spend more time on them,
I could have meetings with PRs and learn about new
products. Everything changed again once I started my
YouTube channel.

Tell us about YouTube.

When I started my YouTube channel, I immediately got
10,000 subscribers as my existing blog readers followed
me on YouTube. My first videos were awful – I was so shy
and monotone. They were about 'What's in my handbag'
and I sound like I'm reading from a script. It just takes
a while to feel comfortable talking on camera. Most
people freeze when the camera comes out and I was no
different – no vloggers are presenters. All we can do is try
to be ourselves. But then I realised it's so nice just to sit and
talk and video really shows your personality in a way that
written posts can't.

What would your advice be to others wanting to get started on YouTube?

Just start! You don't have to show anyone or make it
public until you are comfortable with it.

→

Then it's good to be consistent. I do two videos every week. Think of your YouTube videos as being like a TV show – people like to know when the next episode is coming.

What have been the best things you've done?

I've been photographed by Rankin twice – and I'm not a model. I've become the face of the Teenage Cancer Trust's sunburn campaign. I went to Ghana with Sport Relief on a project that helps women start their own businesses. I've been to New York, Malta, Amsterdam, Paris, Morocco and LA on trips too. But it's not just about me. I have to think how to make a press or brand trip interesting for my viewers. It's about finding the balance between a great opportunity for me and what is good for my viewer. I've turned down some amazing opportunities, but I need to put my viewers first because they're the reason I'm here.

What's your advice to new bloggers and vloggers?

It's scary. You have no manager telling you what you should do and you don't get a pat on the back if you do well. In the first year, only 30 people read my blog each day. I often get emails from new bloggers saying 'no one is reading my blog' and I want to say 'have some patience'. Don't do it for readers – do it because you enjoy it. You can't become a successful blogger overnight. You can't buy your way into it. It all looks easy from the outside, but it's not and you have to be prepared for the fact it takes time.

I'm sure you didn't need convincing about the power of social media, but hopefully you now better understand how it works, what you need to do and the way in which everything in the online world is inextricably linked. It is the power of everything we have talked about from positioning (niches and your personal brand) to traffic to content creation to social media that cumulatively impact on increasing success in all areas of your blog, from the size of your audience to your profile and authority. That's why I'm so keen to present to you the big picture as well as the intricacies. If you are serious about blogging success, for yourself personally or your business (and we're about to talk more about that), then you can't pick and choose one area or the other. You have to do everything.

Chapter 10

Digital footprints for your business

So far in this book, we've mainly been discussing professional blogging and building a blog as a media brand.

But what about blogging for business, either for a company that you own or work for, or for yourself as a professional service provider in a particular niche?

IMAGINE...

... you're a dentist.

That means marketing is tough. Not only do your customers visit you infrequently, some actually find any excuse to avoid you altogether. But people do worry about their teeth, and they do invest in good dental care – so you need to reach out to them even if they're not due for a check-up. You know from your own online experience that your target customers use social media, so ...

You post some high quality content relating to mouth and dental health – helpful but not preaching or promoting – and it gets noticed on social media feeds. You also offer a superbly designed 10-Steps-to-a-Whiter-Smile e-book – and people sign up for it, adding themselves to your mailing list. Now you can send them short, informative, authoritative and encouraging e-newsletters.

See how it works? The people on your list will definitely think of you when they do need a dentist. In the meantime, they'll be telling their friends about you too, helping to build your mailing list even further.

So – if you're a tree surgeon, a plumber, a marketing manager, a lawyer, a property consultant, a professional cleaning company, a horse stud farm … YOU SHOULD BE BLOGGING.

I'm going to say it again. *You absolutely should be blogging for your business.* Your buyers are actively online and you need to be stamping out digital footprints for your business around the web and social media – and blogging is the way to do that. Essentially, whether you invest in your own time or pay someone else to write your blogs, by using the right techniques you will generate more real world sales and attract more customers to your business. Content marketing generates three times as many leads as traditional outbound marketing – and costs less.

And that is true whatever it is that your company does, and whether you are a one-person band or running a large company with hundreds of employees.

Since 2007 I have used, and continue to use, content (including blogging) in all my business activities. Whilst running a company, blogging twice a week brought us more traffic, made us appear more reputable, improved our position in the search engines taking us to the top of Google, made our clients like us and trust us more before they got in touch with us ... need I say more?

And today as a business and digital marketing consultant it's still a central part of my strategy. Without my new content, my website would be dull and static. I use blogs to demonstrate my expertise and bring me all sorts of professional opportunities, ranging from speaking engagements to radio guest slots – to this book.

The internet and digital media have turned the whole business marketing process on its head. Consumers are now actively looking for information, not passively receiving it via advertisements. Business owners need to meet the needs of their prospects and customers by providing helpful, interesting, engaging content in a way that reflects whatever that business has to offer, answers their questions and establishes a trustworthy relationship.

And it gets even better! Look at the overall impact blogging will have on your business:

- You get more leads.
- People recommend you, increasing your content reach.
- You have the best opportunities to communicate your market differentiation.
- You show people what it's like dealing with you.
- You get to state and claim your market authority.
- You build trust and reputational capital.
- You spend less time actually selling – your content brings people to you.

Business blogging – inbound marketing or content strategy – *what's the difference?*

Don't be confused by what different marketing companies might call it – for business purposes it is all effectively the same, all part of creating and sharing valuable free content to engage with an audience of potential customers and turn them into actual customers. Whether you are creating content for a big business or for yourself as a freelance service provider of any sort, you still have an audience made up of those people considering buying your real world products or booking your real world services.

The *type* of content you create is closely related to what you sell, but you are trying to educate, inform and entertain potential and new customers – and in a way that makes them know you, like you and trust you.

Some of the UK's leading business blogs in action

I was really interested to see the final of the UK Blog Awards 2016. Each year, the UK Blog Awards showcases the best of a vast range of blogs, from blogs led by the blog stars we've been reading about, to company blogs.

This year in their company category, the finalists included a huge variety of businesses and organisations, both large and small, household names and local businesses all using content in an inspiring and successful way. Let's hear some of the UK Blog Award finalists in the 'company category' summarise both what their business blog does for their company and customers, and the sorts of topics that they write about.

Cottages & Castles self-catering cottages	Our blog shows another, more personal, side to our self-catering letting business. Although we are holiday accommodation providers, we understand that going on holiday is about the whole experience – where you can go, what you can do and how you can get the most out of your visit. Through fun, informative and interesting content we have built a library of posts which share hints, tips, advice and inspirational stories showing Scotland off as the fantastic holiday destination it is.
The Royal Mint Blog	blog.royalmint.com is the official blog of The Royal Mint. Content on our blog includes: designer interviews, historical articles, guest blogs from our many partners, new coin announcements, bullion news, coin collecting articles, videos, infographics, competitions, interesting facts, the stories behind museum artefacts, blogs from employees across The Royal Mint and much, much more.
Salford Business School	Salford Business School's blog offers a space for academics, students and organisations who work with the school to share their business related lessons, observations and comments. The blog reflects the School's mission for 'Global thinking, Sustainable practice, Industrial collaboration, Professional success' and supports our vision 'to be the primary destination of students and industry for next generation management and law knowledge and practice, that is industry relevant, digitally informed and globally accessible'.

Cancer Research UK	Run by the charity's media team, the Cancer Research UK science blog covers the latest issues in cancer research and care, including research funded by the charity, but also wider issues of relevance to our supporters and the general public. We also debunk myths and media scares, contextualise prominent stories in the headlines and provide links to other helpful resources and information.

Let's look at a brand that's famous around the world and takes business content to an incredible level ...

Now you may have seen the Red Bull name prominently displayed at all kinds of sporting events – and this is because they take their strategy to another level, even putting on their own events to get more film footage. But really, what we are seeing is still part of their enormous content strategy in action.

Don't worry – you won't have to start hiring teams of extreme athletes – but the underlying concept remains the same for any business. It is all about defining your niche (what you are selling) and thinking about what your audience (your potential customers) need to know from you. It's also about differentiating yourself positively from your competition, something that is much easier to do through thoughtful content than blunt advertising.

The good news is that whilst a fashion blogger needs thousands of hits in order to monetise their blog, you need far fewer website visitors for your business blog – just enough of the right visitors to become customers or clients and enable you to grow your business to your ideal size.

Most businesses don't need to appeal to broad consumer audiences, or to everyone. They just need to appeal to those who could become customers. So your content also allows you to communicate your unique differences, approaches and offerings, as Jason Korman from Florida-based business consultancy Gaping Void explains, and end up with fans queuing to work with you rather than customers that you have to try to convince in order to make sales.

Florida-based entrepreneur Jason Korman is a co-founder of Gaping Void, a hugely successful business and training consultancy that uses art to improve its clients' company culture and employee engagement. Their clients are *Fortune 100* firms including HP, Volkswagen, eBay, SAP and Deloitte. At the heart of their consultancy firm is their blog (gapingvoid.com/blog), which has been ranked one of the fifty most powerful blogs in the world and gives them fans instead of customers. They have published 7000 posts about marketing, tech, business and life, and every post includes a cartoon drawn by Jason's business partner, cartoonist Hugh Macleod, which provides a visual way of solving a business problem. The success of their blog also means they now run a retail division which has some 6000 clients buying framed prints of their daily cartoons priced from around $199 each.

Why and when did you start blogging?

We started around 2005, and it was because we were asking ourselves: 'how could we create a business model for a consulting company, how could we get people's attention and how could we engage people from major corporations?' Hugh has a skill-set as a cartoonist and illustrator, so we thought about how to use this meaningfully to attract leads – and we've been relentlessly creating content ever since! We publish a cartoon post six days a week, send out a daily email containing the post, and use social media, especially Twitter, a lot.

How has your blogging strategy impacted your business?

We wouldn't be the business that we are today without it – if we stopped doing it tomorrow, we'd have a lot less new business coming in. Our content is the primary way that we connect with our prospects. It gives us a completely different dynamic to most consulting firms who constantly worry where their next client will come from. For us, people are already fans of our content and style, so we don't have to convince them – they contact us!

Where should business owners start?

The downside today is that there is an ocean of content out there. But if you are smart and have valuable knowledge (which all business owners tend to), this idea of creating really useful valuable content for people is a great strategy for building a business. You just have to make sure you have the right expectations. It doesn't happen overnight. It might take a year, even two years, to get the attention that you want. But whether the results come fast or slow isn't the point – if you want to spread

→

the word about what you do, I don't think there is any other way to do it.

Can content work for established industries?

When you're in an established industry, you have a really interesting opportunity to act differently to the rest of the market and to stand out with your content. We try very hard to do that. And you can't please everyone – there are some firms that would never hire us as they prefer the more traditional consulting firms such as McKinsey or Deloitte. But when people want innovation and real powerful tools for change, they come to us because we are different – and that is what we show them every day with our content.

What is your number one rule?

You have to focus on questions like, 'how will my business help people? How will I do it in a way that justifies my fees?' It's all about them, not about you. Once you've figured out how you will be interesting, you've got to produce content every day. You could do it just once a week, but you are better off doing it twice a week, and every day is best of all. Remember, it's not about traffic when you are blogging for business – it's about the right traffic.

Data collection and email marketing

We talked in Chapter 9 about email marketing as a traffic strategy. But when it comes to a business blog, email isn't just a means of getting more visitors – it's a loyalty and sales strategy too.

The statistics bear this out. Research by the Nielsen Norman Group shows that e-newsletters are still considered a great way to grow or maintain relationships even during times when people aren't actively making purchasing decisions. When it comes to purchases made as a result of receiving a marketing message, email has a higher conversion rate when compared to social media or direct mail.

According to management consultants McKinsey & Co, email remains a significantly more effective way to acquire customers than social media, converting at up to forty times the rate of Facebook and Twitter combined. It brings one of the highest ROIs of all activities that engage and nurture both potential customers and existing customers and, even better, it can be automated.

Let me illustrate once again using my own experience of starting, growing and selling my online press agency business. Our email strategy was significant to us in two key ways.

1. Generating leads: We actively encouraged visitors to the website to sign up for our email list, offering them the 'bribe' that our newsletters would help them learn how to make a little extra money by doing paid interviews with the media. We built up a mailing list of close to 10,000 people and every week we would email them with the latest opportunities to grab some paid media work.

The email list became a huge lead-generator for the

business – but it was a long-term strategy. I was amazed how some of the people who came to us had first joined our mailing list two or even three years earlier. So it took that long to convert a lead into a sale – and if they hadn't been on the list during that time, they might easily have gone to a competitor when they were ready to do business.

2. Selling the business: When it came to selling the business, the email database was considered a major asset, providing valuable access to all the people who had already visited the site and put themselves on the list, or been in touch with the business and opted in to the list at that point. I know that under the business's new owners, the email list continues to grow and generate leads.

How to produce content for a business if you're not a writer

Even if you are now convinced by the benefits of business blogging, you will still need to create content – and much of that will involve writing. So what do you do if you're not confident as a writer?

We looked, in Chapter 7, at ways to find inspiration and write for online readers – and those are relevant for business blogs too, especially techniques such as news hijacking. But I have a few extra tips for business owners.

Firstly, there are plenty of online resources that can help you, such as copyblogger.com and contently.com. Sign up for the newsletter for both and they will send you content creation tips directly to your inbox. But before doing that, have a think about the ideas below – you may discover that writing is a lot easier than you thought, and you will certainly gain an appreciation of how good your content must be.

Take content seriously

Content writing is not a job that can be delegated to a part-time PA or landed on the plate of an already busy employee. It requires thought – and a schedule. Even if you only publish once each week, the week can quickly roll round with the next blog post still unwritten. So take it seriously – make it someone's primary job, or commission a freelancer who will do the job properly and consistently.

Just write

Your content must be of a quality to reflect your professionalism, but nobody is expecting Pulitzer prize-winning journalism. Simply get writing, and write in the same way that you talk. You'll need to edit and refine it, but it will give you a less formal but trustworthy style.

Think about what your customers are asking you ...

... and then write up the answer as a blog post. Remember you are blogging for your customers and potential clients, not for your friends or peers. So think about your customers. Their questions are the best source of inspiration all the time, but especially when you are starting out. Using these topics, you can also extend your thinking to include what *you* would like your customers to know about your business or understand about the industry you operate in.

Use your industry news for inspiration

All industries have their own news, and you can use developments and happenings in your industry to inspire your blog posts, and make you appear like the industry leader you are. Try to be one of the first to offer your comment or opinion on major industry developments, suggestions as to how the industry as a whole can improve. Over time your blog could even become a resource for others in the industry, which will improve your profile as an industry leader. Set up Google alerts for keywords that relate to your industry and use these news stories for inspiration.

Train yourself to see ideas everywhere

Your working world is interesting – it really is! It's just that when you're in the middle of it all every day, you don't see it that way. Showing a glimpse of your world also helps to build that all-important trust. So, look at the things you routinely do, see and say in your business and find the content angle in it. Whenever I work with business owners on their digital strategy, they only need to start talking and my brain will be firing: 'there's a blog post in this', 'there's content in that'.

Forget what you learned at school

Lessons from the past can hold you back when you're trying to write content – after all, you're not writing essays or formal letters. Content needs to be quick to read and easy to scan at a glance. This makes it simpler for you to devise and write content – just create one paragraph for each idea and keep paragraphs short, three or four sentences at most. If you find you can't do this, you're probably trying to write a dissertation, and nobody is going to read that online.

Vary post length

Continuing the previous tip, play around with different lengths of post. Readers appreciate the occasional short statement-like piece of content, especially if it contains just one powerful reflection, thought or piece of advice – and throw in video posts and image-led posts too to shape up the mix.

Pamela Wilson's story includes some useful advice for content creation.

Pamela Wilson is Executive Vice President of Educational Content at Rainmaker Digital, a leading global education organisation teaching content marketing to individuals and brands. Since its launch in January 2006 as a simple one-person blog called *Copyblogger* (copyblogger.com), the company has taught people how to create killer online content that attracts attention, drives traffic, and builds your business. Today, it has 185,000 customers and eight figure annual revenues.

What's the difference between online writing and real world writing?
We consume online content differently, so as content creators we have to write it differently. Reading online information isn't like reading a non-fiction book. Online

→

content is a 'stop by, learn, and move on' type of medium. No one is throwing a blanket over the legs of your online reader, pouring her a warm beverage, and turning on the standard lamp so she can immerse herself in your web page.

So where should people start with their online content?
Start with this fact in mind: you're aiming to create content that makes people pay attention, think, and feel. I believe that remarkable content takes a three-step journey. Start with their eyes. Your reader sees the overall presentation of your information before they read a single word. This means using colours, fonts and formatting to entice them to begin consuming your content. Strong headlines, subheads and solid content will hold their interest. Think about enlisting your readers' hearts – stories that emphasise our common human experiences and emotions are the ones we remember. We all know what it feels like to be bullied or looked down on, we've all felt insecure from time to time and we've all had the experience of working hard and achieving a long-term goal. When you incorporate stories that knit together experiences we've all had, your content will go straight from the eyes to the mind and to the heart – and it will stay there, and be remembered.

What is the structure of an ideal blog post?
Your headline is the most important group of words in your post, so spend plenty of time crafting one that will get the attention you're looking for. The best headlines

feature a promise of what the reader will get from your content – they answer the 'What's in it for me?' question.

Your subheads can branch out from there. Subheads form the backbone of your content: get these right and everything else will flow. Your subheads should be informative enough that someone scanning your post will understand the gist of it. But they should also be intriguing enough that your scanner is left wanting to dig deeper and learn more.

You're talking about 'skimmability' – tell us more.

'Skimmability' isn't really a word – but it should be! I think of it as a quality that makes online content easy to read and consume. Good skimmability involves short paragraphs of 3–4 sentences with the occasional one-sentence paragraph for effect, interesting bullet lists and highlighting specific texts with block quotes.

If you are running a content strategy for a business, how quickly does it work?

Traditional marketing and content marketing have something important in common. In order to get the business results you want – more leads, sales and profits – you have to do them consistently over time. In traditional marketing, you don't place one ad or send out one brochure and think your work is done. In content marketing, you can't write five blog posts or record three podcast episodes and expect them to transform your profits. If you want content to grow your business, you have to produce it regularly.

➔

> **So I can't stop producing content once it's working?**
> No, I recommend you keep it up. Search engines reward sites with fresh content. If you let your content sit there and collect dust, the search engines will move on to other sites with more timely information.

Vlogging for business

You might think that vlogging (or video-blogging) is the preserve of the younger 'YouTube' generation, but remember this – YouTube is the second largest search engine on the globe. It processes three billion searches every month and it's bigger than Bing, Yahoo!, Ask and AOL combined. It's not just an entertainment portal – there are plenty of people out there who prefer video-based, visual information for all kinds of reasons.

So here are the key benefits of vlogging for business.

It puts a human face on a business

Vlogs in which key individuals in the business talk to camera or give a tour around the business premises make a more personal impact on the potential customer. It makes it easier to relate to *you* and imagine doing business with *you*.

It gives a glimpse into the business

Seeing inside your factory or office can also help to build trust – you're literally opening the doors with nothing to hide. I recently worked with a worktop company on their digital strategy and we filmed behind the scenes at their factory, showing worktops being made and the team in action. Almost immediately they received feedback from customers showing that this insight, rather than just videos of the finished article in situ, was what they appreciated most.

Vlogging improves your website's SEO and chances of being found

Google likes to present a mix of media in its search results, so vlogging helps get you more visibility. When vlogging you're putting up new content that you can link to and embed in your blog and all over your social media accounts – and other people can then like and share it, all of which will improve your overall rankings on Google. Embedding your videos from YouTube into your blog also makes your pages more shareable which increases rankings.

Just as you write blog posts based on keywords that people are actually searching, so you should create videos. You can use keywords in the video descriptions or even post transcriptions of the spoken text.

You can repurpose your content for different 'types' of consumers

With a little imagination, many blogs can easily be repurposed as vlogs – and with YouTube being the second largest search engine, you know this will increase your reach. It also means that you're using essentially the same content to cover two distinct bases – those who prefer to read their content and those who prefer to watch videos.

You don't have to be scared of video

Every single person I work with wants to start vlogging and filming for their business. But most don't know where to start with video and feel that things like the editing software must be really difficult to learn because TV professionals make editing sound like some sort of mysterious, cryptic thing. They utter statements like, 'I'm going to be in the editing suite all day Monday so can't answer your call'. Well, as with a lot about life, technology is changing everything and although you might need to be taught video, it's certainly not hard nor beyond you.

It is in response to my clients' needs that I have launched my course 'Lights, Camera, Action: How to Film, Produce & Edit Stunning Showcase Videos For Your Business' which is available on my website.

The impact of business video and vlogging can be huge, as illustrated by this story ...

Graham Hunt is the owner of Spanish estate agency Valencia Property. He began blogging and vlogging at valencia-property.com/new to help his business when it was in deep trouble and the results have been rather extraordinary.

What was the main reason for starting your blog?
In 2006 the Spanish property market was in severe trouble and our sales dropped from 55 that year to eight the year after and just three in 2007. Bearing in mind I

had a team of staff, I was in serious trouble. I had no money to pay for advertising and so started looking at ways to get the business name out there for free – and so I started blogging about buying property in Spain.

When did vlogging come into it?
It began in 2010. I filmed 100 videos over four days, based around the idea of '100 tips for moving to Spain' and I uploaded them one at a time for the next 100 days. It transformed the business and even today those videos, which are now six years old, are still the main thing that get people talking to me and buying property through me. I still film videos of the properties I'm marketing and I'm brutally honest in what I say. If it has a frighteningly steep staircase, I say so. I don't want someone coming over and saying they like it but hate the stairs so won't be buying it, so the vlogs help me market the properties really clearly – and people know I am not bullshitting as I don't just tell them how great the property is.

How has it helped you and your business?
As well as increased sales, the blog also makes my customers loyal and connected to me. Estate agencies have a bad reputation because people don't like or trust us! With the videos, my customers are not meeting me cold. They can see my face on the videos and decide before they come if they like me, whether they trust me and if they want to spend time looking for property with me. They can see I won't be suited and

→

booted like a lot of other agents in the UK and they arrive feeling as though they already know me.

People think YouTube is only full of young people but you show that's not the case.
My clients are usually over forty and fairly well off, but they find me on YouTube. So it can work no matter who your audience is.

Would vlogging to back up a business work for anyone?
I would say it could work for any real world business as long as your sales are fairly high value, and that's only because of the time it takes to film and upload videos. People shouldn't be scared of video. A lot of business owners worry everything has to be as though it's on a TV programme and beautifully photographed, but it doesn't. What people want to see is something real and I give people that.

Make blogging your #1 marketing tool

By focusing on informative and educational content, your business blog becomes your most powerful marketing tool – and that tool has very well defined goals:

- To attract new leads.
- To draw leads to your business website and down your sales funnel.

- To increase customer retention and referral.
- To establish your authority as an industry leader.
- To bring you other business-building opportunities such as speaking engagements, press interviews or book deals.

As I've already outlined, I built my first business on the back of blogging and now use blogging to build and maintain my own profile as I help my clients raise their profiles through digital marketing and publicity. I promise you: blogging for business works in so many different ways and on so many different levels. Make it an absolute priority on your 'to do' list.

Chapter 11

Hitting the wall and other blogging blocks

There is a saying in the online world that 'Most bloggers give up in three to six months; and most of the ones who "make it" simply last longer than the others'.

And yes, starting a blog is the easiest thing in the world; but maintaining it is one of the hardest.

Here's what often happens. You launch with huge enthusiasm, blog for a few months and then suddenly you hit a 'this isn't working' wall. You're creating content that you think is great, but your stats are dismally low, no one is sharing anything and no one is contacting you. That original dream of someday monetising it all seems completely out of reach.

But there's worse. Just as you're experiencing your first doubts, you're also getting overwhelmed by the online world. You get fixated on other people having better websites or photography than you but you don't know how they have done it – and you are considering signing up for endless online courses but you can't afford them.

So you get the blog fear and feel like giving up and going back to the day job. But you're not alone.

Every blogger has hit the wall and felt that their dreams are nothing but delusions and their blog is not going anywhere. It all boils down to one key truth about successful blogging – there is no such thing as an overnight success, a blog takes time and determination to build.

So, in this short chapter I want first to look at some of the things that go badly wrong and bring you to a grinding halt, and then to share a few tips for overcoming this and keeping going when all you feel like doing is giving up.

Four things that can go wrong early on (and how to avoid them)

#1: Agonising over what to write

You know the saying 'One swallow does not a summer make'? Well, how about 'one post does not a blog make'? In fact, make that two posts, three posts, four ...

For your blog to really get traction you are going to create dozens or even hundreds of posts. In the early days, especially, this can be a real challenge as you feel your inspiration ebbing away. Many people experience their first serious doubts at this early stage, but remember what many of our bloggers' stories have shown – early on you *will* only get a few people reading your blog, and many of those will be friends and family. It's part of the process.

So, while I'm not saying you can forget about standards and post any old thing, you should use this time to get into the habit of creating content and finding your voice. Aim for learning, not for perfection. Just type – sit at your computer and write something. Think about what people ask you and then type out the answer. Something is better than nothing. Words that are waffling can be edited into words with meaning. Writing anything is better than staring at a blank screen.

#2: Measuring success too soon

Success at blogging is not measured on a day-to-day basis, especially in the early days. You need to look at a block of time as a whole and assess the opportunities, the highs and the lows you experienced within that period.

So, don't even think about whether your blog is working or not for *at least ONE year!* Whatever today's date is, pick up your smartphone, go to your calendar app and put an alert in it one year from now (or on the day that you launch your blog). That alerts needs to say: 'Is your blog working?'

Having done that, you have given yourself permission *not* to think about it for twelve months – and that's really important because you won't necessarily have reliable feedback in that short time. Just work on your blog.

During the year you will have highs and lows, opportunities will appear – and then suddenly you'll feel as though you are sitting alone in a field of tumbleweed. But even when the alarm goes off, I want you to think back over the year as a whole, not just the day on which the alarm goes off. That's when you should review the entire experience to date – write down how your blog has developed, the opportunities it has brought you and places it has taken you, that you otherwise wouldn't have gone.

#3: Comparing your beginning to someone else's middle or end

Comparisonitis (n): a highly virulent illness that affects people working in the online space. Symptoms include constantly comparing yourself to other bloggers, cringing over the state of your own blog and feeling generally insecure and useless about how brilliant everyone else is and how terrible you are.

Believe me, I've seen so many sufferers of 'comparisonitis' – and there isn't a magic pill that can cure it. There is, however, a therapy for helping you to cope with it and to prevent it sabotaging your blogging.

When you are looking at established bloggers and feeling full of envy, jealousy, fury and other negative emotions that you know you shouldn't feel but just can't help, remember this. You are almost certainly looking at someone who started their own journey *a long time* before you started yours – so of course they're ahead of you!

All the successful bloggers in this book started with low traffic and no income – and their websites may have been redesigned dozens of times along the way to get to what they are now. I for one redesign my website every year or so as I constantly discover new trends and ways to make it all work even better.

So don't compare your start to where they are. Instead, try to feel inspired by their success. There's always someone better than you, so use them as inspiration. All that matters for now is that you keep growing.

#4: Impostor Syndrome

This is another affliction that causes bloggers to quit – and it's to do with the fear of being exposed as a fraud or as not qualified or expert enough. On the outside, everything appears to be going right but on the inside you feel vulnerable, expecting any moment to be 'found out'. For some reason it seems to afflict women more than men.

I definitely experienced imposter syndrome while working as a journalist on a national newspaper as I had never studied journalism or had any interest or ambition to be a journalist, it just kind of happened to me. Even once I'd scored hundreds of by-lines in national newspapers and was running my own online press agency (which often produced front page newspaper stories and which provided jobs to many journalism graduates who have gone on to have sterling careers in journalism), I *still* felt that I wasn't really a 'proper' journalist. It was nothing short of ridiculous!

Even icons like Maya Angelou have admitted to imposter syndrome, saying: 'I have written eleven books, but each time I think, "uh-oh, they're going to find out now".'

But why should it afflict bloggers so much? I think the main reason is something I've touched on several times in the book – it turns the normal career path on its head. It's the opposite of the traditional view of the world where we wait passively to be offered promotions or we have to study and accumulate qualifications before anyone considers our opinions to have validity. As a blogger, you're promoting yourself – and there are no formal qualifications for having opinions.

With blogging, your validation comes within and from your audience – you don't need anyone else's permission or recognition to get started – but you do need confidence, you have to put yourself out there against millions of others, and you have to believe that you're good enough to stay there.

Please don't dismiss impostor syndrome as just a silly insecurity. It's a manifestation of something that happens to us all – comparing ourselves to others in all kinds of ways. Don't tell me you haven't recently looked someone mentally up and down and ranked yourself against them, just to check that you're doing OK or to find out if you need to try harder!

Finally, remember that impostor syndrome is the curse of *all* bloggers. In fact, if you don't experience it, you are probably not sufficiently in touch with what you're trying to achieve. The only way to overcome it, however, is to reduce how much you compare yourself to others, to keep going and to have faith in yourself. If people are reading you, following you and sharing you, and if brands ask you to write reviews, it's all for a reason – you *are* good enough.

Four ways to keep going when you lose momentum

#1: Plan for the long term *and* the short term

In my own life, I have both long-term plans and short-term goals in mind and I try to keep my eye on *both* simultaneously, as focusing on one or the other can prove overwhelming and result in too many questions that I can't answer.

Having a long-term plan is particularly important. Ask any successful expert and they will reveal that they did not know every single step of their journey but they did know where they ultimately wanted to go. They knew the bigger picture, even if they didn't know how exactly they would complete it.

Visualisation is a part of being able to focus on the big picture and long-term goals. I love the saying 'To avoid seasickness, look to the horizon'. That's exactly what visualisation will help you do. So take time to imagine yourself as a successful blog owner. Think of the blog of your dreams, the one you would like to create, and imagine yourself as the owner of it and doing all the things that that particular blog will bring for you.

Your short-term goals are just as valuable – each one takes you a step closer to the long-term goal. Once you've visualised your long-term goal, you find that you can put more of your focus on the smaller ones, the next steps you'll take towards the big one. This means you actually find more quality energy and thought for the smaller details, you resolve small problems more easily, and you find the whole experience a lot more satisfying and less stressful.

#2: Trust the process

If you have read this book chapter by chapter you will know that blogging is a sequential process that involves the following:

- Finding a niche.
- Defining an audience.
- Setting up your blog.
- Content creation.
- Social sharing and conversation.
- Listening and learning from your audience.
- And doing the content creation and social side of things over and over again.

As a process it has a start, a middle and, if or when you choose it, an end. It is not an overnight metamorphosis, but a journey. And it's a very well-mapped journey. Some of the results are predictable, others will be a surprise, but as a process it is proven – all of our bloggers have done it. Trust in it. It works. So follow it.

#3: Just do it!

Procrastination will get you nowhere. The only way to even begin to get successful with blogging is to jump right in and start. If you've *already* been running a blog but it's stagnant and going nowhere, then use what you've learned in this book to kick-start it. Get writing, get creating content, make it a priority and just sit down and do it.

As Mark Twain said: 'The secret to getting ahead is getting started.'

#4: No excuses permitted

Blogging is dynamic – so you must be too. There is no room for excuses – 'I'm busy, I'm not feeling my best, I just need to wait for a really great idea for my next post . . . ' You need to acquire a 'This is happening right now' mentality and make blogging a priority.

We all have the same twenty-four hours in each day and excuses are just your attempt to rationalise why you are giving up on whatever blogging dream you had. So, stop it. Get up at 5am. Stop watching TV. Prioritise. Most of the bloggers here began alongside a full-time job but the reason they succeeded is because they prioritised their remaining time – they made time to blog, and they kept blogging.

I suggest you come back to this chapter when you spot those first signs that you may be slowing down – we all need reminding from time to time. And take some comfort from Sean's story below. He didn't give up – and it's certainly paid off for him!

Sean Evans, twenty-four, from Stoke-on-Trent, is the founder of *Back to the Movies* (bttm.co.uk), a world-famous film blog that is ranked in Vuelio's 'Top Ten Most Influential Film Blogs'. Since its launch Sean, who previously →

worked in marketing for a gas calibration company, has worked on over fifty films, interviewed stars, walked the red carpet at the BAFTAs, transformed his blog into a trusted brand and resource on all things movie-related, and become friends with leading Hollywood stars.

Tell us about *Back to the Movies*, why did you start it?
When I was twenty-one, I had this idea of making something memorable to mark my 21st birthday – something to look back on in a few years' time. So I went on Google and scrolled through various celebrities whose work I enjoyed, actors such as Richard Kiel who played Jaws in *James Bond* and Jeremy Bullock from *Star Wars* and, using their websites, email, Twitter or whatever I could find, I got in touch with them and asked them to send me a birthday message. I wasn't expecting anything, but I actually got video messages back from Bill Moseley from *Devil's Rejects*, and Dick Warlock from *Halloween II*, and I thought: 'These people have replied so quickly, how easy would it be for me to set up a page where I could actually interview them and talk about their films?'

A few months later, *Back to the Movies* started! The main idea behind it came from me being sick of seeing the same sort of generic interviews on TV. My hope with my Skype interviews was the ability to have intimate interviews where people would be in their own homes, offices and environments without any restrictions. So I started to do these interviews, and everyone was so free-flowing and relaxed that it came across like a conversation rather than a professional interview.

Did it take off straight away?

Not at all. Traffic was terrible. I had ten visitors per day, and half of them were my brother and my girlfriend. You begin to question yourself, thinking: 'why aren't people reading it? Is my writing and spelling that bad?'

My first breakthrough was when I contacted the team making an independent film called *6 Degrees of Hell*. I explained I had a marketing background and asked them if they wanted me to promote their film on my blog. They did and my name was included in their credits. However, I was still only getting 50–60 hits per day. It was still disheartening to see.

So how did you keep going?

I had to adopt a mentality of perseverance – if you really want something and are really passionate about it, you've got to keep going. Even if I just went up by one hit a day, it's still one hit more than the day before. I also had this vision of turning the blog into a brand – I'd get a studio film, I'd get a news outlet to cover it – and I wasn't going to stop until I got there. It was tough as I was still working full time for the first two years of blogging.

When did you reach a 'turning point' moment?

In 2013. I approached a crowdfunding campaign in which James Franco was raising money for a film project of his called *Palo Alto Stories*, and they offered me an interview with him! One email later, I was on Skype with James Franco, talking about *Palo Alto Stories*. It ended up being covered by the *Hollywood Times*, the *LA Reporter*,

→

The Wrap and *Made TV*. But what clinched it was that all the interviews would say, 'when speaking to Sean Evans of *Back to the Movies*'. It got picked up on Yahoo and BT, and almost overnight I started to generate a lot more traffic.

Around the same time, I noticed that an independent horror film called *Fear Clinic* was being made, starring Robert Englund (who played Freddy Krueger). I reached out to the writer of the movie, Aaron Drane, enquiring about work on the movie as Robert's autobiography *Hollywood Monster* was one of the books that inspired me to take the leap into self-employed work in the movie industry. I was then on the project and flown out to Los Angeles to work on the movie and then met up with Robert for a nice dinner with his lovely wife Nancy in Laguna Beach.

So your site generates opportunity in the real world too?
Yes, it's a mix. With *Fear Clinic*, I did their blogging, advertising and running all their social media pages and content. I started reaching out to similar small, independent firms – the kinds of people with a budget up to around £15 million. They were always so grateful for the promotion, so would almost always reply and be happy to chat. In the beginning, I did that for free but I've since worked on marketing campaigns for over fifty independent films and am paid as a consultant. The films like the fact that not only do I know the digital world and help them generally, but I can also promote their film to my own audience who love independent films.

Meanwhile, the blog has gone from being updated every 3–4 days to being updated six times a day. I've done some incredible things: one minute I'm writing a blog, here in my house in Stoke-on-Trent in the UK, the next I'm in LA or attending the BAFTAs in London as a VIP guest!

Would you say your journey has been easy?
No – the idea that bloggers don't have to work is false. If you really want to achieve something and get where you want to be, you have to work hard. If you want to do it as a hobby you can do it in your own time, but if you want to do it as a job you've got to put the hours in because you've got a lot of competition. I've worked hard to be in the privileged position I am, and to be enjoying the prestigious experiences that it brings.

It's your time – seize it!

'If I have seen further than others, it's by standing upon the shoulders of giants.'

ISAAC NEWTON

I hope you have found the individual stories inspiring – hearing directly from hugely successful men and women across the blogosphere, blogging for all different reasons and in all different niches, some earning significantly more than a million dollars a year, some whose blogs have now become their main business and some who use their blog to drive huge growth in their existing business.

These stories will continue to provide inspiration. Each time you *reread* them, you will notice different themes and details standing out. You've absorbed the complete picture now and can better relate to those steps and hurdles that each person experienced in their unique journeys.

But there's one more thing to do – start

Until you do, it will all remain theoretical – and the best way to learn is on the job.

You will see now that there is a process to successful blogging. There are things you must do: knowing your niche, developing your personal brand, creating content and excelling at social media.

But one thing I've learned more clearly than ever from talking to the bloggers in this book is that the path to a million dollar blog is not a linear one – you can't 'blog-by-numbers' following a set series of steps. The way the internet works, and will continue to evolve, is too fluid for that.

In fact, I suspect there is no other industry in which the path to riches is both so clear and yet simultaneously so unclear. All successful blog owners have mastered everything we have talked about, yet at the same time they have cumulatively shown us that there is no one way, not of doing things or even of bringing in income.

But you have one advantage none of our bloggers had ...

You have this book. They didn't. That means that you *begin* with an overarching view of the blogosphere – you will be embarking on your journey with more knowledge and understanding of the small systems and big picture than they ever did.

Yes, the blogosphere is more crowded and noisy than ever and will only continue to grow. But I guarantee you that in the years to come there will be many more 'big name' bloggers emerging and ever-increasing opportunity to work with brands. Why shouldn't you be one of them?

It's not just a game of fame and celebrity

Blog stars *are* the celebrities of the future. But if you choose to blog to grow your business, that will bring success that is worth celebrating too. You should now understand why blogging for business is not just desirable – it's essential. You can't afford NOT to be online. It's where your customers are right now – and the internet will only become even more ingrained as the only serious way to learn about products and services, glamorous or not!

What are you waiting for?

Armed with the knowledge and information you now have, it's time to start.

By reading this book, your thoughts will be more focused and your sense of direction will be clearer, but you won't have all the answers. No one ever does – and that's fine, it's the way the game is played. You learn as you go along. But you can't begin to learn until you start.

Don't wait, don't over-analyse, don't paralyse yourself with pro-crastination and definitely don't wait for permission from anyone else. Don't be scared, don't be shy, don't worry about the whats, the hows and the whens.

Commit to content creation and commit to making your dream a reality. It's not a get-rich-quick scheme – it's a journey. But if you embark on that journey properly, you can build the same success as the people we have met in this book. I promise you that.

So get out there and get started – and let me know how you get on.

Index